kitchen
stitches

sewing projects to spice up your home

COMPILED BY KAREN M. BURNS

Martingale®
Create with Confidence

Kitchen Stitches: Sewing Projects to Spice Up Your Home
© 2014 by Martingale & Company®

Martingale
19021 120th Ave. NE, Ste. 102
Bothell, WA 98011-9511 USA
ShopMartingale.com

Printed in China
19 18 17 16 15 14   8 7 6 5 4 3 2 1

Library of Congress Cataloging-in-Publication Data is
available upon request.

ISBN: 978-1-60468-403-2

Mission Statement

Dedicated to providing quality products and service to
inspire creativity.

Credits

PRESIDENT AND CEO: Tom Wierzbicki
EDITOR IN CHIEF: Mary V. Green
DESIGN DIRECTOR: Paula Schlosser
MANAGING EDITOR: Karen Costello Soltys
ACQUISITIONS EDITOR: Karen M. Burns
TECHNICAL EDITOR: Ellen Pahl
COPY EDITOR: Sheila Chapman Ryan
PRODUCTION MANAGER: Regina Girard
COVER AND INTERIOR DESIGNERS: Paula Schlosser
and Connor Chin
PHOTOGRAPHER: Brent Kane
ILLUSTRATORS: Christine Erikson and Sue Mattero

contents

Introduction

*I*f you're like many sewists and quilters, you like to cook almost as much as you like to play with fabric. Even if cooking isn't high on your list of favorite activities, you've probably found that your family, friends, and guests love to gather in your kitchen, and with good reason. The kitchen is the heart of the home; it's where we go to find nourishment (or sometimes just a good cup of coffee), be creative (experimenting with a new recipe, perhaps), and make memories (Thanksgiving wouldn't be the same without Grandma's apple pie recipe). Now you can make this favorite space even more special with colorful, practical designs that say, "Welcome to my kitchen."

We asked a few of our favorite designers for their best ideas, and the result is this fabulous collection of bright, pretty, fun-to-sew projects. You'll love the pieces that help you "Get Cooking" (page 5), from easy pot holders and aprons to unique quilted cozies—one for a casserole and one for a slow cooker. (Hint: They make awesome shower gifts!)

Whether you're entertaining guests or enjoying family dinner, you'll want to "Set the Table" (page 45) in style. Place mats, napkins, tablecloths, and table runners are so easy and fun to make, you can make new ones for every season (or each time an irresistible new fabric line comes out). And just for fun, "Add a Little Spice" (page 77) to your home with handmade memo boards, fridge magnets, and coasters. They're quick to make from scraps and they make great hostess gifts.

So whether you're a gourmet cook or a take-out speed dialer, whip up a couple of fresh fabric treats to make your kitchen warm and welcoming!

Mary V. Green
Editor in Chief

get cooking

french-farmhouse chef
Apron, Basket Liner, and Baguette Tote

*T*here's nothing like a walk through a farmer's market to inspire a meal with friends. To make sure the golden crust of your fresh bread isn't crushed by a jar of local lavender honey, take along a tote made especially for carrying baguettes.

Set a lovely table for a French-farmhouse dinner using thick handblown glasses, rustic plates, and the richness of woven linen, including the coordinating breadbasket liner. As guests arrive, greet them in a handmade linen apron to match the evening's ambiance.

apron

Designed and made by Natalie Barnes.
Fabric by Robert Kaufman Fabrics.
Finished size: 30" wide x 40" long (one size fits most)

Materials

Yardage is based on 42"-wide fabric.

1¼ yards of natural linen
3 yards of ¼"-wide black grosgrain ribbon
1½ yards of 1½"-wide black grosgrain ribbon

Cutting

From the linen, cut on the *lengthwise grain*:
1 piece, 32" x 42"
1 strip, 2½" x 42"; cut into:
   1 strip, 2½" x 26"
   1 strip, 2½" x 16"
2 strips, 1" x 42"

Assembling the Apron

1. Fold the large linen piece in half lengthwise so it measures 16" x 42". Press the center fold lightly to create a placement guide for centering the ribbon.

2. Measure 6½" from the top center fold and mark along the top edge. Measure 14" down from the top-right corner along the open edges of the fabric and mark the distance. Using a rotary cutter and long ruler, trim off the two top corners, cutting from mark to mark.

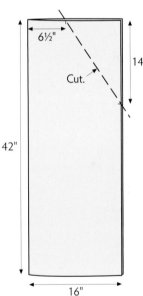

3. Open up the apron and pin the 1½"-wide grosgrain ribbon to the center of the apron body using the crease as a guide. Using dark thread in the needle of your machine and light thread in the bobbin, stitch close to the edge of the ribbon on both sides. Test your tension first to be sure the light thread doesn't show through to the top of the dark ribbon. Remove pins as you sew to avoid stitching over them. Pin a length of ¼"-wide grosgrain ribbon on each side of the wider ribbon,

½" away. Stitch close to the edge of the ribbon on both sides.

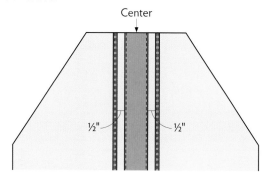

4. To hem the lower left and right sides of the apron, turn under ½" to the wrong side and press. Turn under ½" again and press. Stitch close to the inner folded edge.

5. For the neck strap, fold the 2½" x 26" linen strip right sides together; stitch using a ⅜"-wide seam allowance. Turn the fabric tube right side out with the seam along one side and press.

Stitch.   Press.

Straight Stripes

In the make-do world of French-farmhouse life, this apron might be made from a repurposed tablecloth of striped linen. For this version, Natalie created her own stripes using woven grosgrain ribbons. To keep the narrow ribbons straight and parallel to the center ribbon, measure over from the edge of the wider ribbon ⅝" at several points down the apron front and make a dot. Using a pencil, draw a line connecting the dots and center the ribbon over it as you pin.

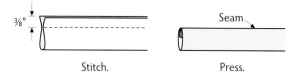

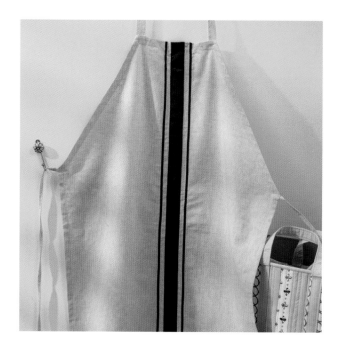

6. Place the neck strap on the right side of the apron with the seam edge toward the center of the apron and the outer edges of the strap ends 1" in from the outer edges of the apron. Baste or pin in place.

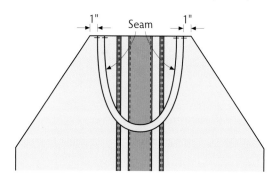

7. Place the 2½" x 16" linen strip right sides together at the top of the apron. Baste or pin in place and stitch using a ⅜"-wide seam allowance. Press the seam allowances toward the facing.

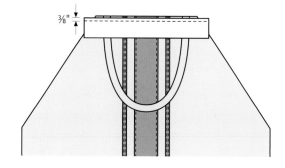

8. Turn the raw edge of the facing under ¼" and press. Turn the facing to the wrong side of the apron and press. Trim the edges of the facing even

with the angled apron sides and stitch the facing to the apron close to the folded edge. Stop stitching when you reach the ribbon and backstitch. Skip over the ribbons and begin stitching again, backstitching to secure the seam, and sew to the edge of the apron. Stitch the unsewn section of the facing by hand.

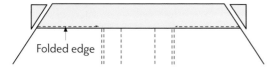

Folded edge

9. To hem the angled upper sides of the apron, press under ½" to the wrong side. Turn under ½" again (or up to the edge of the neck strap) and press. Stitch close to the inner folded edge.

10. To hem the apron bottom, press under 1" to the wrong side. Turn under 1" again and press. Stitch close to the inner folded edge.

11. With wrong sides together, press the 1" x 42" linen strips in half lengthwise. Open up each strip, fold both edges in to the center fold line, and press. The strips should now measure ¼" wide. Stitch through the center of each folded strip to make the apron ties.

Center fold

12. Turn under the raw edge of each apron tie ½". On the wrong side of the apron, align the ties with the intersection of the hemmed sides and upper angled edges of the apron. Stitch along all four sides, encasing the raw edges. Stitch an X in the center of the stitching to finish. Tie a knot in each end of the ties for style points.

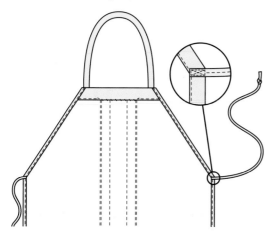

basket liner

Designed and made by Natalie Barnes.
Fabric by Robert Kaufman Fabrics.
Finished size: 7"-diameter base; 18"-long wraps

Materials

Yardage is based on 42"-wide fabric. Fat quarters measure 18" x 21". Fat eighths measure 9" x 21".

⅝ yard of natural linen
1 fat quarter of print for liner bottom
5 fat eighths of assorted prints and solids for liner*
10" x 10" square of batting
10" x 10" square of Insul-Bright

*If you're making more than one of the French-Farmhouse projects and want to use matching fabrics, purchase fat quarters.

Cutting

See "Custom Fit" on page 10 to modify the cutting for your basket.

From the fat quarter, cut:
1 circle, 9" diameter

From *each* of the fat eighths, cut:*
1 strip, 2½" x 12"
1 strip, 2" x 12"
1 strip, 1" x 12"

From the linen, cut:
2 strips, 8" x 42"; cut each strip in half crosswise to yield 4 pieces, 8" x 21"
1 strip, 2½" x 42"

From the batting and Insul-Bright, cut *from each:*
1 circle, 9" diameter

*You'll have more strips than you need, but this will give you the opportunity to vary the fabric layout and sizes of the strips. Use the leftover pieces to make coordinating projects, if you like.

Custom Fit

Natalie's basket was 7" in diameter at the bottom. For a different size, measure the diameter of your basket and add 2" when cutting the circles. Add 1" to the width of the flaps for every 1" increase in the diameter of the basket. For example, if your basket is 9" in diameter, cut 11" circles and cut the linen strips 10" wide (8" + 2").

Assembling the Basket Liner

The base of the basket liner is constructed using the "quilt-as-you-go" technique, which means you'll be quilting the layers as you add each new piece of fabric. If you've never used this technique, read the tips in "Quilt-As-You-Go Method" on page 11 first.

1. Place the circle fabric right side down. Layer the batting and then the Insul-Bright on top and baste the layers together with safety pins.

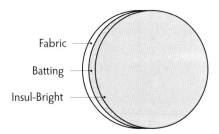

Fabric
Batting
Insul-Bright

2. Select one of the 12"-long strips of fabric (any width) and place it right side up, just off center on your layered circle. Remove any safety pins that will be in your way when sewing the strip to the

layers. Pin the strip in position with quilter's pins if you like, but the fabric should stick to the Insul-Bright and is less likely to shift.

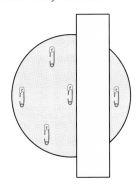

3. Fold a scrap of fabric to make a scrap starter or leader. Natalie likes to make two: one for the beginning and one for the end. Begin sewing on the scrap of fabric, and then continue to the strip. Quilt a vertical line through the strip and all layers. Rotate your piece and quilt another row in the opposite direction. Change direction with each line of quilting to ensure your piece will remain round. The number of lines you quilt into each strip will depend on the width of the strip and your personal preference.

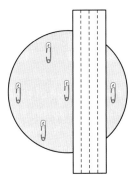

4. Place a second 12"-long strip right sides together with the strip you just quilted, aligning the raw edges. Sew together through all layers using a ¼" seam allowance. Flip open the new strip and finger-press, or press with an iron.

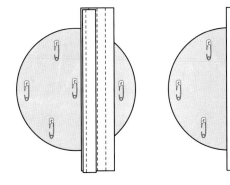

5. Quilt through all layers as before, keeping the quilting lines parallel to those in the first strip.

6. Repeat steps 4 and 5, varying the strip widths and colors and varying the spacing of the quilting lines, until the entire circle is covered.

7. Make a 7" circle template (or the diameter of your basket) and trace it onto your quilted circle. Trim the circle.

8. Hem the two long sides and one short side of each 8" x 21" linen strip by folding under ¼" to the wrong side two times and pressing. Stitch close to the inner folded edge.

9. Place the quilted circle on the short raw edge of a linen strip. Mark the arc of the circle on the linen with a pencil. Trim along the marked line. Repeat for all four linen strips.

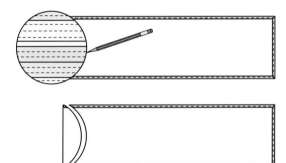

10. Pin the wrong side of one linen strip to the strip-pieced side of the quilted circle at the twelve o'clock position. Stitch using a scant ¼" seam. Repeat with a second linen strip at the six o'clock position. Sew the last two strips to the circle at the three o'clock and nine o'clock positions.

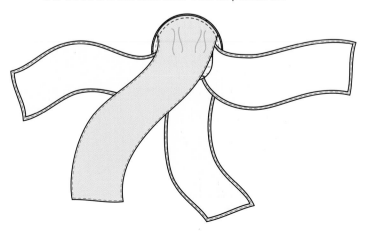

11. Fold the 2½" x 42" linen strip in half lengthwise, wrong sides together, and press to make the binding. Attach the binding to the raw edges of the circle over the linen flaps, leaving a 2" to 3" tail at the beginning. Sew slowly and carefully with a ⅜" seam allowance. Be mindful of the linen strips as you sew; hold the fabrics flat while attaching the binding. As you near the starting tail, fold the edges of the starting tail under ¼". Trim the binding end and insert it into the beginning. Complete the stitching and whipstitch the binding ends together where they overlap. Stitch the binding to the back of the circle by hand.

Quilt-As-You-Go Method

With this method, you quilt the layers together as you sew your strips together. Take your time and treat each component of your project as you would a quilt.

- Cut backing fabric and batting 2" larger than the finished piece; you'll place strips over these pieces, sew, and trim your project to size after you've finished quilting and adding strips.

- Baste all layers together using rustproof safety pins.

- Prepare your machine by lengthening the stitch and inserting a new quilting or top-stitching needle.

- Use a walking foot for best results.

- Check the tension by sewing on some scraps of your fabric and batting first.

- If your machine has the option, reduce the presser-foot pressure.

Cutting

From the lining print, cut:
2 rectangles, 12" x 25"
1 strip, 2" x 42"; crosscut into 2 strips, 2" x 21"

From the canvas, cut:
2 rectangles, 12" x 25"
2 strips, 1" x 36"

From *1* of the assorted fat quarters, cut *along the 20" length:*
2 strips, 2½" x 20", for binding
1 strip, 3" x 20"
1 strip, 2½" x 20"
1 strip, 2" x 20"
1 strip, 1" x 20"

From *each* of the remaining 4 fat quarters, cut *along the 18" length*:
2 strips, 3" x 18"
2 strips, 2½" x 18"
2 strips, 2" x 18"
2 strips, 1" x 18"

From the linen, cut:
2 strips, 4" x 36", for handles
2 strips, 2½" x 42"; crosscut into 2 strips, 2½" x 26", and 2 strips, 2½" x 16"

Making the Tote Sides

You'll construct each side of the tote using the quilt-as-you-go technique. Refer to "Quilt-As-You-Go Method" on page 11 for helpful hints.

1. Place a 12" x 25" rectangle of lining fabric right side down on your work surface. Add a 12" x 25" rectangle of canvas on top, and then a batting rectangle. Baste the layers together using safety pins or by hand with a needle and thread.

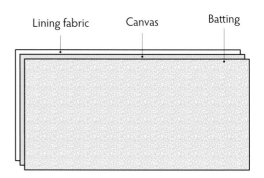

baguette tote

Designed and made by Natalie Barnes.
Fabric by Robert Kaufman Fabrics.
Finished size: 24" x 11"

Materials

Yardage is based on 42"-wide fabric unless otherwise noted. Fat quarters measure 18" x 21".

⅞ yard of print for tote lining
½ yard of natural linen for tote sides, handles, and binding
5 assorted fat quarters for tote sides
½ yard of 100% cotton 7-ounce canvas, 54" to 60" wide, for tote interior
2 rectangles of lightweight 100% cotton batting, 12" x 25"
Quilting or topstitching sewing-machine needle
Walking foot

2. Sort the strips cut from the lining fabric, fat quarters, and linen into two piles so that you have approximately 20 strips in each (one for each side of the tote).

3. Select one strip of fabric and place it right side up just off center on the batting layer. Remove any basting pins that might be in the way. The strips will be longer than needed; trim the ends even with the batting as you go.

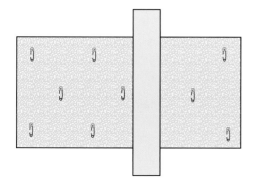

4. Using a leader (a folded scrap of fabric sometimes called a scrap starter), stitch through the fabric strip and through all layers with a vertical line parallel to the 12" side of your piece. End your stitching with a second leader; snip the threads between the leader and the layered piece and remove the layered piece from the machine. Rotate it and sew a second line through the strip. Continue quilting lines through the strip until you like the look. The number of lines you quilt in the strip will depend on the width of the strip and your personal preference. Stitch in opposite directions from one line of quilting to the next to ensure your piece will remain square.

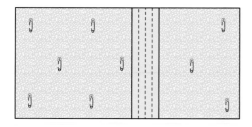

5. Choose a second strip and place it right sides together with the strip you just quilted, aligning the raw edges. Sew together through all layers with a ¼" seam allowance. Flip open and finger-press, or press with an iron. Trim the ends even with the batting.

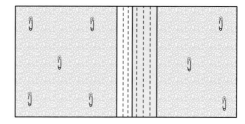

6. Stitch quilting lines parallel to the first piece, changing direction as you did before.

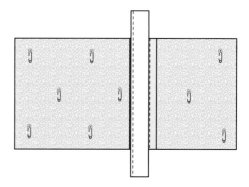

7. Repeat the process to add strips, varying your strip widths and colors and varying the distance between quilting lines, until the whole piece is covered.

8. Repeat steps 1–7 to prepare the second side.

Variation Is Key

Vary your strip widths, fabric colors, and spacing between quilting lines to make your project more interesting.

Assembling the Tote

1. Trim the tote sides to measure 24" x 11". Cut the left and right sides at an angle by measuring in 7" from the bottom corners as shown. Then draw a line to the upper corners and cut through all layers along the line.

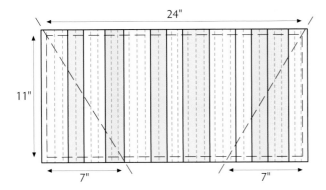

2. Prepare the linen binding for each tote side by folding the 2½" x 42" strips in half wrong sides together; press. Sew the binding to the long strip-pieced sides of the tote using a ¼" seam allowance. Turn the binding to the inside and stitch by hand.

3. For the handles, fold the linen 4" x 36" strips right sides together; press. Place a 1" x 36" strip of canvas in the fold. Fold the left and right edges of the linen strip into the center fold, encasing the canvas, and press. Measure in 10¾" from each end of the handle and stitch through the center of the handle as shown, reinforcing the ends of the stitching with an X. Make two handles.

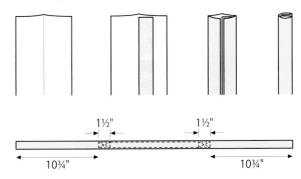

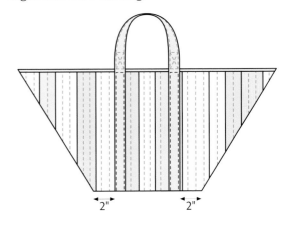

4. Place and pin a handle on each tote side, 2" from the lower corners and keeping the open edge toward the center of the bag. Stitch close to both edges below the binding.

5. Place the tote sides together, with lining sides facing each other. Pin along the edges, catching only one layer of the second tote side. This will keep the pieces flat. Machine baste ¼" from the sides and bottom of the tote.

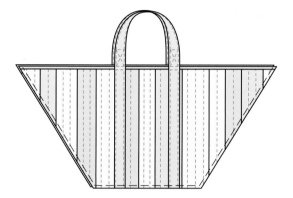

6. Prepare the binding using the 2½" x 20" strips. Sew them together using a diagonal seam and then fold wrong sides together and press.

7. Attach the binding to the tote along the basted edges, leaving a short tail at the beginning and end. Sew slowly and carefully using a ⅜" seam allowance, the quilting or topstitching needle, and a walking foot. Miter the corners referring to "Crisp Miters" at right. Turn in the raw ends of the binding strip so that they encase the raw edge. Turn the binding to the other side and stitch by hand.

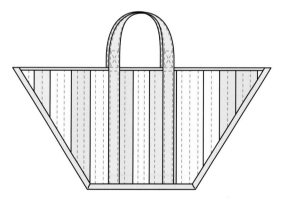

Crisp Miters

For a crisp mitered corner when binding anything other than a 90° angle, follow these simple guidelines.

1. Stitch up to the intersection of the ¼" seams and backstitch. Remove the piece from the machine.

2. Fold the binding up so that the folded edge of the binding and the next raw edge of the quilted piece are aligned.

3. Fold the binding down to align the raw edges of the binding and the quilted piece. Make the fold at the corner.

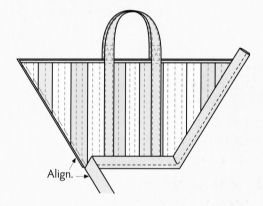

Align. →

4. Begin stitching at the folded edge and continue to sew the binding to the quilted piece.

vintage-inspired kitchen:
Casserole Cozy and Double-Handed Pot Holder

*M*any quilters are also collectors—and in addition to our fabric stash, we often have glassware, cookware, dishes, and more. You can change the look of your kitchen with a simple shuffle of collections—and by adding some sewn accessories. Start with a large-scale focus print that pulls in the colors of your collectibles. Add some small-scale coordinating prints and solids, and your projects will create a whole new look in your kitchen without having to remodel.

casserole cozy

Designed and made by Natalie Barnes.
Fabric by Robert Kaufman Fabrics.
Finished size: 13¼" x 24" (to fit a 9" x 13" casserole dish)

Materials

Yardage is based on 42"-wide fabric. Fat quarters measure 18" x 21".

⅔ yard of large-scale print for backing and binding
6 coordinating small-scale print fat quarters
2 coordinating solid fat quarters
18" x 36" piece of batting
18" x 36" piece of Insul-Bright
1 button, 1" diameter

Cutting

See "Recipe for Dimensions" on page 18 if your casserole dish is larger or smaller than 9" x 13".

From the large-scale print, cut:
1 strip, 15¼" x 42"; crosscut into:
    1 rectangle, 15¼" x 26"
    1 rectangle, 9½" x 15¼"
2 strips, 2½" x 42"

From *each* of the 8 fat quarters, cut:*
2 strips, 3" x 18"
2 strips, 2½" x 18"
1 strip, 2" x 18"
1 strip, 1" x 18"

From the batting and Insul-Bright, cut *from each:*
1 rectangle, 15¼" x 26"
1 rectangle, 9½" x 15¼"

*You'll cut more strips than needed, but this will give you the opportunity to vary the fabrics and sizes of the strips.

Sewing and Quilting the Cozy

You'll construct the cozy using the quilt-as-you-go technique. Refer to "Quilt-As-You-Go Method" on page 11 for helpful hints.

1. Place the large-scale print 9½" x 15¼" fabric right side down on your work surface. Add the 9½" x 15¼" piece of Insul-Bright (following the manufacturer's instructions), and then the batting. Baste the layers together using rustproof safety pins or by hand with a needle and thread.

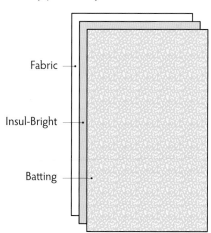

Fabric

Insul-Bright

Batting

Recipe for Dimensions

To adjust the dimensions to fit any baking-dish size, measure the length and width of your dish along the top, including any handles. Measure the depth and record your numbers. Be aware that measuring the outside of the dish will give you a different dimension than the size of the dish printed on the bottom; that is the size specified in recipes. Natalie's classic 9" x 13" baking dish measures 9¼" x 14½" at the top.

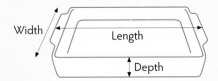

Follow the steps below to calculate the finished sizes for the flap and bottom. You'll add 2" to these dimensions for the size to cut and quilt. After quilting, trim to the finished sizes and follow the steps for finishing.

1. Add two times the depth of the dish to the measured width for *finished width*. The width is the same for the flap and bottom. For example, if your dish is 2" deep, add 4" to the width.

2. For the flap, subtract 3" from the measured length to allow for the gap at the top (for buttoning up the cozy). Divide this number by two and you'll have the finished *flap length*.

3. For the bottom, add two times the depth to the length; then add the flap length calculated in step 2. This is the finished *bottom length*.

4. For the flap, use the width from step 1 and the length from step 2. Add 2" for the size to cut.

5. For the bottom, use the width from step 1 and the length from step 3. Add 2" for the size to cut.

2. Select one of the fat-quarter strips and place it right side up on the layered unit, aligning the 15¼" edges. Remove any basting pins that might be in the way. The strips will be longer than needed; trim the ends even with the batting after quilting each strip.

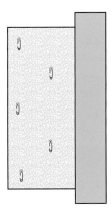

3. Using a leader (a folded scrap of fabric sometimes called a scrap starter), stitch through the fabric strip and through all the layers with a vertical line parallel to the 15¼" side of your piece. End your stitching by continuing to stitch onto a second leader; snip the threads between the leader and the layered piece and remove the

piece from the machine. Rotate it to begin sewing from the opposite direction and sew a second quilting line through the strip. Continue quilting lines through the strip until you like the look. The number of lines you quilt into each piece will depend on the size of the piece and your personal preference, but don't make them so close together that your cozy becomes too stiff to use. Stitch in opposite directions from one line of quilting to the next to ensure your piece will remain square.

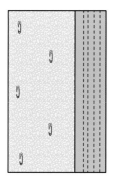

4. Choose a second strip and place it right sides together with the strip you just quilted, aligning the raw edges. Sew together with a ¼" seam allowance through all layers. Flip open and finger-press, or press with an iron. Trim the edges even with the batting. Stitch quilting lines parallel to the first piece, changing direction as you did before.

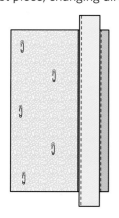 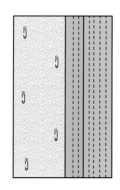

5. Repeat the process to add strips, varying the strip widths and colors and varying the distance between quilting lines, until the entire 9½" x 15¼" piece is covered.

6. Repeat steps 1–5 to prepare and stitch the 15¼" x 26" pieces of fabric, Insul-Bright, and batting for stitching. When quilting the 15¼" x 26" piece, place the first strip of fabric in the center of the 26" length and quilt. Add additional strips to the right, and then to the left.

Finishing

1. Trim and square up the 9½" x 15¼" piece to 7½" x 13¼". Trim and square up the 15¼" x 26" piece to 13¼" x 24".

2. Select an organizing fabric (see "The Well-Dressed Kitchen" tip on page 20) from the remaining strips to use as a binding around the opening. Cut one strip, 2½" x 13½"; fold with wrong sides together and press. Use this strip to bind one 13¼" side of the 7½" x 13¼" piece. Fold the binding to the wrong side and stitch by hand.

3. To make a loop for the button, cut a 1" x 6½" strip from the same organizing fabric. Fold in half with right sides together and press. Open and fold the raw edges in toward the center; fold and press again. Stitch close to the double-folded edge. Pin the loop to the unpieced side of the 13¼" x 24" piece, centering it along one short edge.

4. Place the 13¼" x 24" piece with the unpieced side up; place the 7½" x 13¼" piece on top, strip side up and with the raw edges matching. Baste in place.

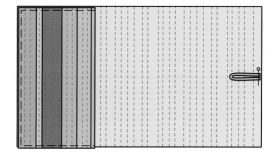

5. Prepare the binding using the two large-scale 2½" x 42" strips. Sew them together using a diagonal seam, fold wrong sides together, and press. Attach the binding to the outer edges of the cozy. Sew slowly and carefully, using a walking foot and a scant ⅜" seam allowance. Turn the binding to the back and stitch by hand.

6. Sew the button on the outside of the 7½" x 13¼" flap, centering it along the edge, so that you can secure the flap and snug up your cozy.

The Well-Dressed Kitchen

To coordinate accessories for your kitchen, use an *organizing fabric.* This is a fabric that you use again and again in your project, or in multiple projects, in a specific role. You could also call it a focus fabric. For a string quilt, it might be the center strip. For a Log Cabin quilt, it might be the center square. For this cozy, it could be an orange print used for the binding at the opening and for the loop. Or in a subtler manner, it could be the same fabric used for the lining and the binding. It says, "I'm a well-thought-out design." It's like a matching handbag and shoes that coordinate with your outfit.

double-handed pot holder

Designed and made by Natalie Barnes.
Fabric by Robert Kaufman Fabrics.
Finished size: 8" x 30"

Materials

Yardage is based on 42"-wide fabric. Fat eighths measure 9" x 21".

¾ yard of large-scale print for backing and binding
6 coordinating small-scale print fat eighths
4 coordinating solid fat eighths
18" x 36" piece of batting
18" x 36" piece of Insul-Bright

Cutting

From the large-scale print, cut:
2 strips, 9" x 42"; crosscut into:
    1 strip, 9" x 32"
    2 rectangles, 8" x 9"
2 strips, 2½" x 42"

From *each* of the small-scale prints and solids, cut *along the 9" length:*
2 strips, 3" x 9"
2 strips, 2½" x 9"
2 strips, 2" x 9"
2 strips, 1" x 9"

From the batting and Insul-Bright, cut *from each:*
1 piece, 9" x 32"
2 pieces, 8" x 9"

*You'll cut more strips than you need, but this will give you the opportunity to vary the fabrics and strip widths.

Sewing and Piecing the Pot Holder

You'll construct the pot holder using the quilt-as-you-go technique. Refer to "Quilt-As-You-Go Method" on page 11 for helpful hints.

1. Place a large-scale 8" x 9" fabric piece right side down on your work surface. Add an 8" x 9" piece of batting, and then the Insul-Bright (following the manufacturer's instructions). Baste the layers together using safety pins or thread baste with a sturdy needle and white thread.

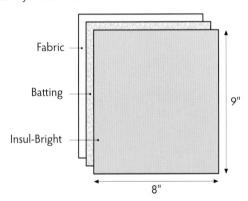

Fabric

Batting

Insul-Bright

9"

8"

2. Select one of the fat-eighth strips and place it right side up, aligning the edges with the 9" side of your layered fabric, batting, and Insul-Bright. Remove any basting pins that might be in the way. The strips will be longer than needed; trim the ends even with the batting as you go.

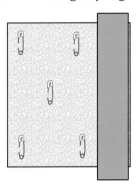

3. Using a leader (a folded scrap of fabric sometimes called a scrap starter), stitch through the fabric strip and all the layers with a vertical line parallel to the 9" side of your piece. End your stitching with a second leader and remove the layered piece from the machine. Rotate it and sew a second line through the strip. Continue quilting lines through the strip until you like the look. The number of lines you quilt into each piece will depend on the width of the strip and your personal preference, but don't make them so close together that your pot holder becomes too stiff. Begin stitching in opposite directions each time you sew a line of quilting to ensure your piece will remain square.

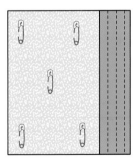

4. Choose a second strip and place it right sides together with the strip you just quilted, aligning the raw edges. Sew together with a ¼" seam allowance through all layers. Flip open and finger-press, or press with an iron. Stitch quilting lines parallel to the first piece, changing direction as you did before.

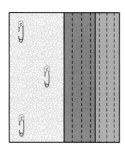

5. Repeat the process to add strips, varying your strip widths, colors, and distance between quilting lines, until the entire 8" x 9" piece is covered.

6. Repeat steps 1–5 to prepare the second 8" x 9" piece and the 9" x 32" piece. When quilting the 9" x 32" piece, place the first strip of fabric in the center of the 15" length and quilt. Add additional strips to the right, and then to the left.

Finishing the Pot Holder

1. Trim the 8" x 9" pieces to 7" x 8". Trim the 9" x 32" piece to 8" x 30".

2. Using an 8"-diameter circle template or a saucepan lid that measures 8" across, mark rounded corners on both ends of the 8" x 30" piece and one 8"-side of each 7" x 8" piece. Trim.

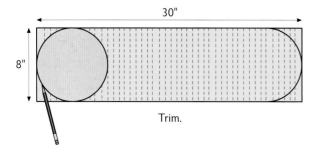

30"

8"

Trim.

3. Select an organizing fabric (see page 20) from your remaining strips to use as binding for the small pieces. Cut two strips, 2½" x 9"; fold them wrong sides together and press. Use these strips to bind the remaining 8" side of each 7" x 8" piece. Fold the binding to the wrong side and stitch by hand. Trim the excess binding even with the edges.

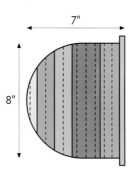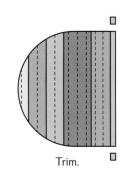

7"

8"

Trim.

4. Place the 7" x 8" pieces on the large-scale print side of the 8" x 30" piece. Baste in place using safety pins through just enough layers to secure the pieces.

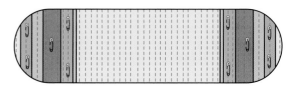

5. Sew the two 2½" x 42" strips together using a diagonal seam to make one long strip. Fold it wrong sides together and press. Attach the binding to the oven mitt. Sew slowly and carefully, using a walking foot and a ⅜" seam allowance. Turn the binding to the back and stitch by hand.

slow-cooker cozy

W hat's not to love about coming home to a homemade meal already cooked? But if you're like Rebecca and find the cord and the bulky base unit always seem to be in the way, try her recipe for this Slow-Cooker Cozy. It holds the lid in place, and prevents burnt fingers during serving or transport.

Designed and made by Rebecca Silbaugh.
Fabric from Simply Style by V and Co. for Moda.
Finished size: 11" diameter x 5½" high (to fit a 5-quart round slow cooker)

Materials

Yardage is based on 42"-wide fabric.

⅞ yard of print for outside of cozy*
⅞ yard of print for lining of cozy
½ yard of solid for binding
36" x 45" piece of lightweight cotton batting
1 yard of Insul-Bright
Basting spray
½ yard of elastic, ⅛" wide
¾ yard of elastic, ¼" wide
3 buttons, ¾" diameter
Removable fabric marker

*Rebecca used a stripe with varying width zigzags.

Cutting

Refer to "Sizing Alternatives" on page 26 before cutting if your slow cooker is a different size or shape.

From *each* of the print fabrics, cut:
1 piece, 9" x 42"
1 piece, 18" x 20"

From the batting and Insul-Bright, cut *from each*:
1 piece, 9" x 42"
1 piece, 18" x 20"

From the solid fabric, cut:
2½"-wide bias strips to total 130"

Preparing the Bottom and Sides

1. Place the 9" x 42" print piece for the outside of the cozy right side down. Add the 9" x 42" pieces of batting and Insul-Bright, and then add the lining print right side up. Spray baste the layers together. Repeat for the 18" x 20" pieces.

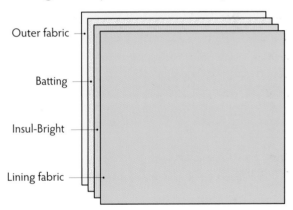

Outer fabric

Batting

Insul-Bright

Lining fabric

2. Machine quilt through all the layers of each piece. It might help to lengthen your stitch length while quilting due to the thickness. The quilting doesn't need to be fancy; it can be a grid of straight lines using a walking foot or a simple allover free-motion design using a darning foot. Rebecca quilted lines following the stripes of her fabric.

3. Trim each 9" x 42" piece to measure 6" x 37" (or the dimensions you need for your slow cooker; refer to "Sizing Alternatives" on page 26 to determine specific measurements).

4. Trace the bottom of your slow cooker onto the quilted 18" x 20" piece with a removable fabric marker. Rebecca likes to use Sewline air-erasable

pens. Trim around your markings, adding 1" all around. (If you have a plate that's a bit larger than your slow cooker, you can trace around that instead.) From the remaining quilted piece, cut two 4½" squares.

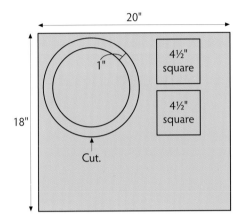

5. Stitch the binding strips together and press them in half, wrong sides together. Attach binding to three sides of each 4½" square piece. Fold the binding over and stitch it down by hand.

6. Wrap the quilted side snugly around your slow cooker and pin in place so that the end falls about halfway between the slow-cooker handles.

7. Pin each of the 4½" squares in place just under the handles, aligning the raw edge of the square with the top raw edge of the quilted side. These squares will create flaps that serve as "pot holders" when picking up the slow cooker. Place them

with the matching fabric facing out, or vice versa if you want the lining print to show as a contrast to the sides of the cozy.

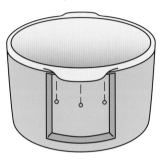

8. Remove the slow cooker and lay the cozy out flat. Cut three 6" pieces of ⅛" elastic and make loops by pinning the raw edges to the outer raw edge of the quilted side piece. Pin one elastic loop in the center of the side and the other loops 1" above and 1" below the first loop.

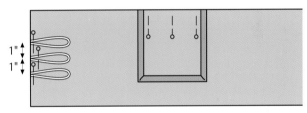

9. Cut two 13" lengths of ¼" elastic and make loops by pinning the ends on each side of the 4½" squares. Be sure not to twist the elastic.

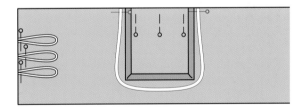

10. Machine baste the elastic loops and the 4½" squares in place, removing the pins as you sew.

11. Stitch the binding onto the quilted side piece, securing with it the loops and squares. Bind only the two short sides and top edge of the piece; backstitch as you sew over the elastic pieces to anchor them securely in place.

12. Fold the binding over to the lining side and stitch by hand.

Constructing the Cozy

1. To attach the side to the bottom, place the pieces with outer fabrics facing each other. Begin with the bound edge with elastic loops and slowly work your way around the bottom, pinning and easing the side to match the contour of the bottom. The side is larger than the bottom; it will wrap around and overlap the beginning edge. Stitch the pieces together, sewing slowly and using a slightly longer than normal stitch length and a generous ¼" seam allowance.

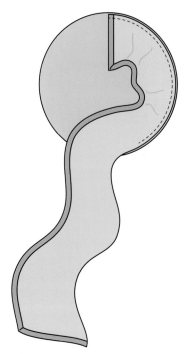

2. Finish the interior of the cozy by attaching binding to cover the raw edges of the seam that joins the side to the bottom. Fold the binding over and stitch it by hand. You may find it helpful to turn the cozy inside out for this step.

3. Measure over from the small elastic loops and mark where the buttons need to be added. You'll want the elastic taught but not tight. Insert the slow cooker to test the placement of the buttons before sewing them on.

4. Sew on the buttons; now you're ready to cook!

Sizing Alternatives

What if your slow cooker is a different shape or size? Follow the guidelines below to determine the finished sizes of the side, bottom, and squares. After determining the finished sizes, add a couple inches all around so that you begin with larger pieces and trim them to size after quilting.

Bottom: Measure the diameter of your slow cooker and add 1". For oval or rectangular shapes, measure the length and width and add 1" to each dimension.

Side: Measure the circumference or distance around and add 5".

Height: Measure the height (to the lip if anything protrudes) and add ½".

Pot-holder flaps: Measure the width of the handle, and then measure the distance from under the lip to a comfortable spot above the lid for the length.

modern pot holders

*T*hese pot holders are a fun optical illusion. Although they look like oven mitts, you can't put your hand in them! The pot holders shown here are made from Log Cabin blocks, but you can use any large "orphan" blocks you have on hand. They're also a perfect project for using up scraps.

Designed and made by Jenifer Dick.
Finished size: 7" x 11"

Materials for One Pot Holder

Scraps of medium-blue solid, dark-blue solid, yellow-green solid, green solid, and blue print for the block*

10" x 14" piece of green solid for backing
10" x 14" piece of Insul-Bright
Freezer paper

*OR one completed quilt block, from 9½" to 12" square. See "Using an Orphan Block" on page 29 for additional details.

Batting Alternative

Insul-Bright, an insulated batting, can be found at most large fabric stores and quilt shops. If you can't find it, double up on regular batting.

Cutting

The cutting instructions that follow will result in a block very similar to the one that Jenifer made. Feel free to improvise the cutting to create your own random-pieced Log Cabin block.

From the dark-blue solid, cut:
1 square, 1½" x 1½"
1 strip, 1" x 5½"
1 strip, 1½" x 4"
1 strip, 2½" x 9½"

From the yellow-green solid, cut:
1 rectangle, 1" x 1½"
1 rectangle, 1" x 2"
1 square, 2" x 2"
1 rectangle, 2" x 3½"

From the green solid, cut:
1 rectangle, 3" x 5"
1 strip, 1½" x 7½"
1 strip, 2½" x 10"

From the blue print, cut:
1 rectangle, 2½" x 3½"

From the medium-blue solid, cut:
1 strip, 1½" x 6½"
1 strip, 3" x 9"

Assembling the Block

Press all seam allowances away from the block center after adding each strip. For each round, begin at the top and work in a clockwise direction.

1. Add the first round of strips cut from the yellow-green solid. Sew the 1" x 1½" piece to the top of the dark-blue 1½" square. Add the 1" x 2" piece to the right side. Sew the 2" square to the bottom and sew the 2" x 3½" piece to the left side.

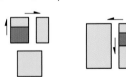

2. For the second round, sew the blue-print 2½" x 3½" piece to the top of the unit from step 1. Add the dark-blue 1" x 5½" strip to the right side. Sew the dark-blue 1½" x 4" strip to the bottom and the medium-blue 1½" x 6½" strip to the left side.

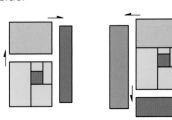

3. To add the third round, sew the green 3" x 5" piece to the top of the unit from step 2. Add the medium-blue 3" x 9" strip to the right side. Sew the green 1½" x 7½" strip to the bottom and the green 2½" x 10" strip to the left side.

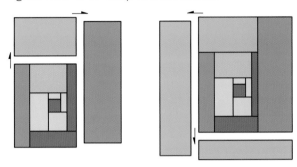

4. Complete the block by sewing the dark-blue 2½" x 9½" strip to the bottom. The block should measure 9½" x 12".

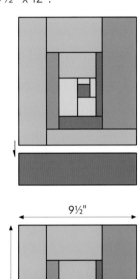

Using an Orphan Block

Your block needs to measure at least 9½" x 12". If you have a 9½" square block, you can simply add a 3" x 9½" strip to the bottom to bring it up to size. For a 10½" square block, add a 2" x 10½" strip to one side.

Assembling the Pot Holder

1. Trace the patterns on pages 30 and 31 onto the dull side of freezer paper to make a template.

2. Press the template to the green-solid backing fabric and cut out on the line. If you use a print for the backing, press the template to the wrong side of the fabric. Remove the freezer paper.

3. Layer the Insul-Bright, Log Cabin block, and mitt-shaped backing with the backing on the top. (If you used a print backing, layer it right sides together with the block.) Peek under the backing to make sure the Log Cabin block is where you want it. Try several placements before you decide.

4. Once you're happy with placement, pin along the edges to keep the three layers from shifting while you sew.

5. Sew around the raw edges of the backing using a ⅜" seam allowance. Leave about 3" open on the straightest side for turning. Backstitch at the start and stop.

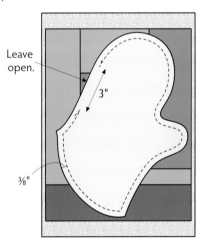

Smooth Stitching

Use a walking foot to sew the three layers together. It will keep the layers from slipping, especially as you sew around the curves.

6. Trim the layers even with the backing and carefully clip the inner curves. Be sure not to clip into the stitching. It's a good idea to clip the Insul-Bright separately from the fabric so that you have more control.

7. Turn the pot holder right side out. Push the corners out and along the curves with a blunt-tipped tool such as a wooden stiletto.

8. Press the pot holder and whipstitch the opening shut with thread that matches the background.

9. You can add machine stitching if you like, or consider it done and put it to good use in your kitchen right away. If you add any quilting, use a walking foot to keep the layers from shifting as you sew.

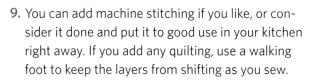

Pot-holder top
Cut 1 from green solid fabric.

⅜" seam allowance

Join pattern at this line.

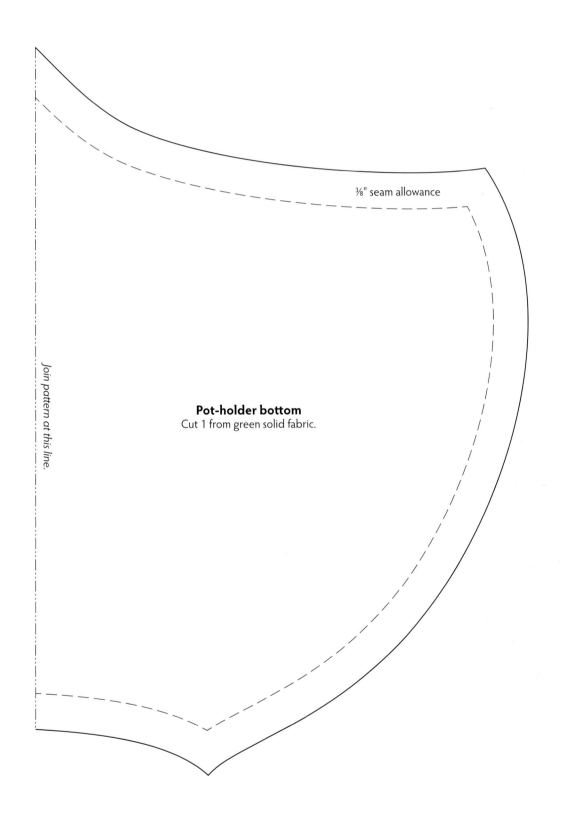

⅜" seam allowance

Pot-holder bottom
Cut 1 from green solid fabric.

Join pattern at this line.

terrific towel

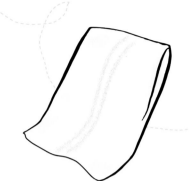

*K*itchen towels can be elusive—they slip and slide around and occasionally you may find them on the floor. With this towel, there's no more slipping—all you have to do is tie it to your oven-door handle (or wherever it would be useful) and you'll always know where to find it.

Designed and made by Linda Turner Griepentrog.
Finished size: 16" x 26"

Materials

Yardage is based on 42"-wide fabric.

1 kitchen towel (linen, cotton, or terry cloth)*
¼ yard of print #1 for border
¼ yard of print #2 for casings
2¼ yards of grosgrain ribbon, 1" wide, for ties
1½ yards of jumbo rickrack
Fray preventer (optional)

Prewash the towel to avoid subsequent shrinkage and potential color transfer.

Cutting

From print #1, cut:
1 strip, 4" wide x ½" longer than width of towel

From print #2, cut:
2 strips, 2½" wide x ½" longer than width of towel

Making the Border

1. Stitch the rickrack along the long edges of the print #1 strip, aligning the points with the fabric raw edges.

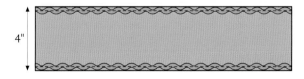

2. Press the rickrack to the wrong side of the border, extending the points. Press under the short border ends ¼".

3. Pin the border in place on the towel, 3½" from the lower edge.

4. Stitch around all four edges of the border with matching thread and a straight stitch.

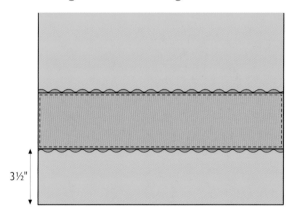

Easy Basting

Instead of pins, you can hold the border fabric in place with a glue stick or fuse the edges with a narrow strip of fusible web.

33

Making the Casing

1. Press under ¼" on all four edges of the print #2 strips for the casings. Stitch the hem along the short ends.

2. Measure the loose circumference of where you plan to hang the towel—oven door, dishwasher handle, etc.—and note this number. (The towel shown allows 5¾".)

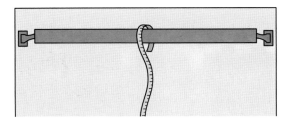

3. Fold under 6" to 7" along the upper edge of the towel and drape the towel where you plan to hang it to audition the distance between the casings. Unfold the towel and pin one casing 2½" from the upper edge. Pin the second casing edge the measured distance apart, noting that the measurement goes to the center of each casing. Try the towel again to check the casing positioning.

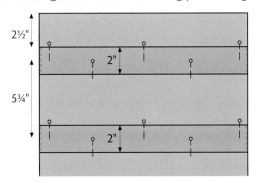

4. When you're happy with the placement, edge-stitch the long edges of the casings in place, backstitching at each end.

5. Cut two 40" ribbon lengths and use a safety pin to thread one through each casing. Trim the ribbon ends diagonally. Apply fray preventer if desired.

6. Fold the ribbons and towel in half vertically and pin-mark the center points. Stitch through the casings for ¼" at each center point to keep the ribbons from pulling out of the casings.

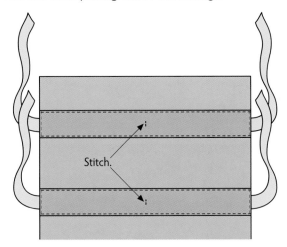

Stitch.

7. Fold the top of the towel over the handle you're using and tie the ends of the ribbons together.

Sous-Chef Trio
Pot Holders and Dish Towel

*B*eing safe doesn't mean you can't also be fabulous! Choose your favorite prints to make a statement in the kitchen—or an easy-sew gift for your favorite sous chef. The pot holders are heavy duty, making them perfect for cast-iron pots and pans. Use the scraps to decorate a coordinating dish towel.

sassy, happy pot holders

Designed and made by Kim Niedzwiecki.
Finished size: 7¼" x 8¼"

Materials for One Pot Holder

Yardage is based on 42"-wide fabric. Fat eighths measure 9" x 21".

1 fat eighth *each* of 3 prints for pot-holder front, back, and lining*
⅓ yard of black print for bias binding
10" x 20" piece of lightweight cotton batting
10" x 20" piece of Insul-Bright
Freezer paper

**You can use 3 Layer Cake squares or scraps that are 10" x 10".*

Cutting

From the fat eighths, cut *a total of*:
2 rectangles, 8" x 9½" (lining and back)
1 rectangle, 7" x 8" (front)

From the black print, cut:
2½"-wide bias strips to total 38"
1 strip, 2½" x 9½"

From the batting and Insul-Bright, cut *from each*:
1 piece, 8" x 9½"
1 piece, 7" x 8"

Assembling the Block

1. Assemble a "sandwich" of the 8" x 9½" pieces of fabric, batting, and Insul-Bright, placing the fabrics facing right side out on the top and bottom of the layers. Layer the 7" x 8" pieces so that the fabric is right side out on the top, the batting is next, and the Insul-Bright is on the bottom with the flannel side facing out.

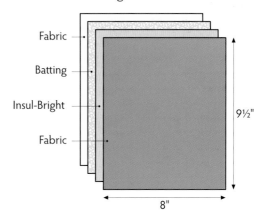

2. Baste the layers together with safety pins and quilt by machine using a walking foot for straight lines or a darning foot for curves and free-motion designs.

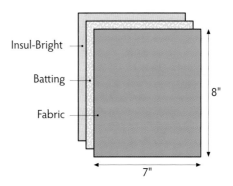

3. Make templates by tracing the patterns on page 41 onto freezer paper. Use them to cut a pocket from the 7" x 8" quilted piece and cut a pot holder from the 8" x 9½" piece.

 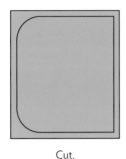

Cut.   Cut.

4. Sew around the edge of each piece to reinforce the edges for long use.

5. Make binding using the 2½" x 9½" strip. Fold it wrong sides together along the length and press. Sew the binding to the pocket piece along the straight edge of the Insul-Bright. Turn to the front and stitch along the edge by machine.

6. Place the pocket, fabric side facing out, onto the pot holder and pin into place.

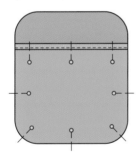

7. Make binding using the 2½" bias strip and sew to the edges of the pot holder along the pocket side. Turn to the back side and sew by hand.

too-hot-to-handle pot holders

Designed and made by Kim Niedzwiecki.
Finished size: 3" x 5¾"

Materials

Assorted scraps for pot holder
1 piece of fabric, 7" x 8", for lining (or use scraps)
1 strip of fabric, 2½" x 10", for binding
7" x 8" piece of Insul-Bright
7" x 8" piece of lightweight cotton or wool batting
Freezer paper

Cutting

From the scraps, cut:
10 to 12 strips, 1" to 2" wide x 4" long

From the lining fabric, cut:
2 rectangles, 4" x 7"

From the Insul-Bright and batting, cut *from each:*
2 rectangles, 4" x 7"

Assembling the Handle Holder

1. Sew the assorted scrap strips together using ¼" seams to make two rectangles approximately 4" x 7". Press seam allowances to one side.

2. Make a four-layer "sandwich" with the pieced rectangle, batting, Insul-Bright, and lining rectangle. The fabric pieces should both be facing right side out on the top and bottom. Make two.

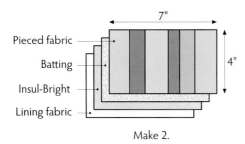

Make 2.

3. Baste the layers together with safety pins and quilt by machine using a walking foot for straight lines or a darning foot for curves and free-motion designs.

4. Make a freezer-paper template using the pattern at right. Press the template to the quilted rectangle and cut a pot holder. Repeat for the second quilted rectangle.

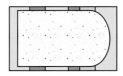

5. Fold the binding strip in half with wrong sides together and press. Using a ¼" seam, attach binding to the short straight edge of each pot-holder unit. Flip the binding to the other side and secure by hand or machine.

6. Layer the two quilted units with right sides together and sew around the curved edges using a ¼" seam. Backstitch at the beginning and end.

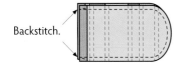

Backstitch.

7. Turn the holder right side out and topstitch ¼" from the curved edges, backstitching at the beginning and end.

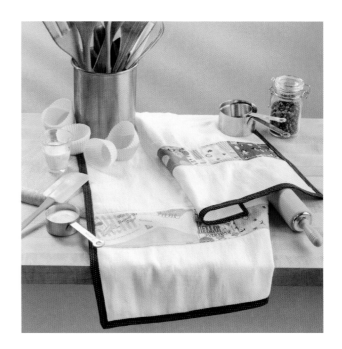

not-for-guests-only dish towel

Designed and made by Kim Niedzwiecki.
Finished size: 15" x 26"

Materials

1 flour-sack tea towel*
½ yard of chenille, terry cloth, or woven cotton fabric for backing
Scraps of 3 prints for accent border (or 1 strip, 3½" x 15")
Fabric scrap, approximately 4" x 8", for hanging strap
¼ yard of dark print for binding

These can often be found in inexpensive sets of 5.

Cutting

Wash, dry, and iron the tea towel and fabric before cutting.

From the tea towel, cut:
1 rectangle, 15" x 23"

From the print scraps, cut:*
1 rectangle, 3½" x 7½"
1 square, 3½" x 3½"
1 rectangle, 3½" x 5"

From the fabric scrap for hanging strap, cut:
1 rectangle, 3½" x 7"

From the backing fabric, cut:
1 rectangle, 15" x 26"

From the binding fabric, cut:
3 strips, 2½" x 42"

Feel free to cut and piece the accent border from scraps as you like. The border should measure 3½" x 15" after piecing.

Assembling the Towel

1. Measure 7" up from the bottom of the towel and cut across the center.

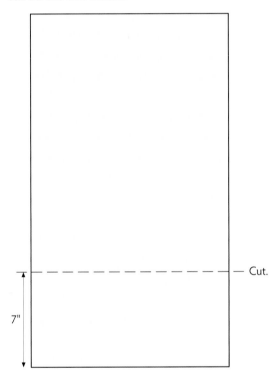

— Cut.

7"

2. Sew the scrap 3½" rectangles and squares together to make an accent border that's 3½" x 15".

3. With right sides together, sew the pieced accent border to the upper section of the towel using a

¼" seam allowance. Sew the border to the bottom section of the towel. Press the seam allowances toward the accent border.

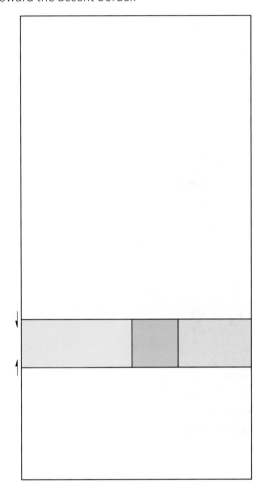

4. Place the towel wrong sides together with the backing fabric and pin into place.

5. Topstitch the accent border ¼" from each side of the seam lines.

6. To make the hanging strap, fold the 3½" x 7" piece of fabric in half with wrong sides together and press. Open up the strip and fold the raw edges in to the center; refold along the center and press again. Stitch along the open side ¼" from the edge.

Center fold →

¼"

7. With the back side of the towel facing you, place the strap diagonally in the upper corner. Pin in place, baste along the edges, and trim the excess.

8. Make binding using the 2½" x 42" strips and attach to the front of the towel. Turn to the back and stitch by hand or machine.

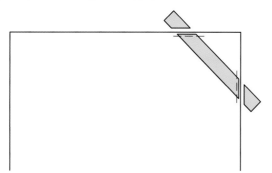

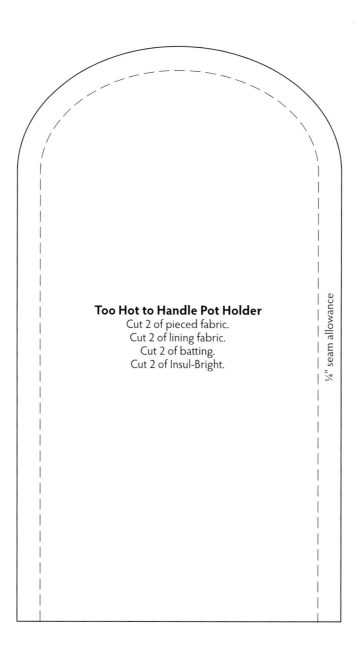

Too Hot to Handle Pot Holder
Cut 2 of pieced fabric.
Cut 2 of lining fabric.
Cut 2 of batting.
Cut 2 of Insul-Bright.

¼" seam allowance

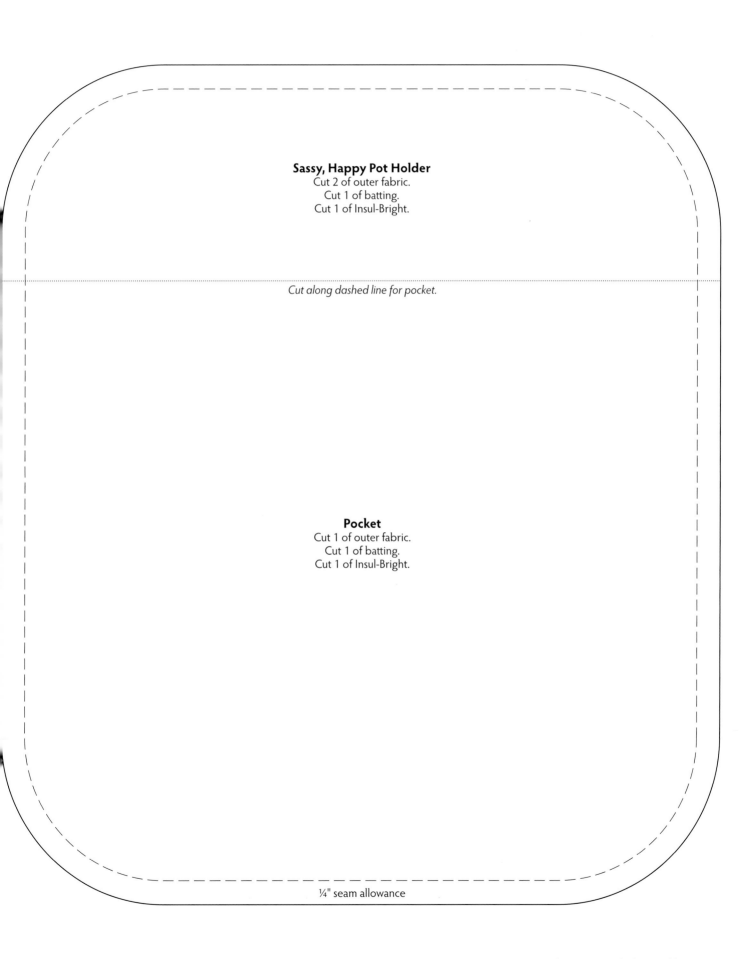

Sassy, Happy Pot Holder
Cut 2 of outer fabric.
Cut 1 of batting.
Cut 1 of Insul-Bright.

Cut along dashed line for pocket.

Pocket
Cut 1 of outer fabric.
Cut 1 of batting.
Cut 1 of Insul-Bright.

¼" seam allowance

shirt tales apron

*R*epurpose a men's button-down shirt into a totally practical cooking cover-up. Using the original shirt details, it's a snap to make—the collar, buttonholes, and placket are already done.

Designed and made by Linda Turner Griepentrog.
Finished size: 29½" long at center front

Materials

1 large or extra-large men's button-down shirt
1 yard of medium rickrack*
⅓ yard of ½"-wide fusible-web tape
Fray preventer (optional)

*Check the center-front shirt measurement to determine exact amount needed.

Cutting

Refer to "Cutting the Shirt" below before cutting the ties.

From the shirt back or sleeves, cut:
2 strips, 3½" x 25", for ties

Cutting the Shirt

1. Lay the shirt out flat and cut off both sleeves. Determine the natural shoulder line (there may be a portion of a yoke showing on the shirt front) and press a crease. Cut away the shirt back at the crease and at the side seams.

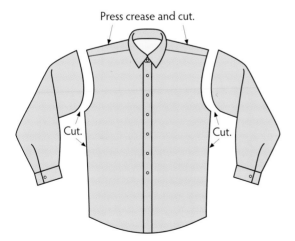

Press crease and cut.

Cut.   Cut.

2. Carefully trim along the lower edge of the back of the collar band, being careful not to cut into the band itself.

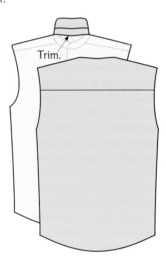

Trim.

3. Using a long clear ruler and rotary cutter, trim the shirt beginning at the collar to just below the armhole. The exact angle will depend on the shirt construction.

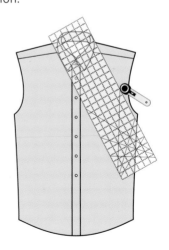

Constructing the Apron

1. Press under a ¼" hem along the angled "armhole" edges, being careful not to stretch the bias edges. Fold under another ¼" and stitch in place, tapering to nothing at the back neckband.

2. Position the rickrack just under the front placket edge and topstitch in place, turning under the ends at the top and bottom to prevent fraying.

3. Fuse the shirt-front placket closed below the last button, keeping the lower edges even. Follow the manufacturer's instructions to adhere the fusible-web tape.

4. Fold the 3½" x 25" strips in half, right sides together, and stitch the long edges and across one end using a ½" seam. Trim the corner, turn right side out, and press to make the ties.

5. Press under a double ¼" hem along the side edges of the shirt. Tuck the raw ends of the ties into the fold, just below the armhole edge. Topstitch the hem in place.

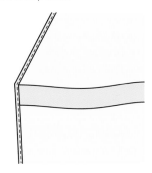

6. Turn the tie outward and stitch again to reinforce.

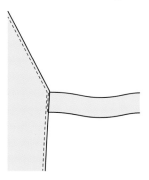

7. If the back neckband lower edges show signs of fraying, apply a fray preventer product and/or trim closer to the band.

One Step Beyond

Use the leftover shirt fabric to add pockets, a ruffle, or a fabric flower to the apron. Or, make matching hot pads and add matching trim to kitchen towels.

set the table

circle blooms tea cozy and place mats

*T*his set of matching tea cozy and place mats features bright circles of reverse appliqué peeking through a beautiful natural linen fabric. Hand-embroidered stitches accent the circles. A bit more embroidery on the tea cozy brings the circles to life as lively, cheerful blooms. So set your table for tea and cake, and bring the garden indoors!

tea cozy

Designed and made by Amy Struckmeyer.
Finished size: 12" wide x 10" high

Materials

Yardage is based on 42"-wide fabric.

½ yard of natural linen (or cotton) for exterior
½ yard of teal print for lining and appliqué
⅛ yard of gray print for binding
5" x 10" piece of orange print for appliqué and tab
5" x 5" piece of yellow print for appliqué
12" x 30" piece of Insul-Bright
4" x 12" piece of lightweight fusible interfacing
Embroidery floss in teal, orange, yellow, and
 light green
Needles for embroidery and hand sewing
Removable fabric marker or chalk
6" embroidery hoop (optional)
Spray starch or starch alternative (optional)
Cardstock

Sized to Fit

This tea cozy was designed to fit a standard four-cup teapot. Amy used a teapot about 4½" tall by 9" long (from end of handle to tip of spout). If you want the cozy to fit a larger teapot, simply enlarge the tea cozy template as needed, but keep the circle appliqué design at the original size.

Cutting

Make a paper template using the pattern on page 52.

From the linen, cut:
2 using template

From the teal print, cut:
2 using template
1 square, 4" x 4"

From the orange print, cut:
1 rectangle, 3" x 5"
1 square, 4" x 4"

From the yellow print, cut:
1 square, 4" x 4"

From the gray print, cut:
1 strip, 3" x 42"

From the Insul-Bright, cut:
2 using the template

From the interfacing, cut:
3 squares, 3¾" x 3¾"

Applying the Reverse Appliqué

1. Center and fuse one square of fusible interfacing to the wrong side of each of the three print 4" squares.

2. Starch and press one linen exterior piece. This is helpful for holding the shape of the fabric while stitching the appliqué.

3. Make templates from cardstock using the circle patterns on page 51. On the right side of the pressed linen, trace two A circles and one B circle

using a removable marking pen or chalk. Follow the placement guide or place the circles as desired.

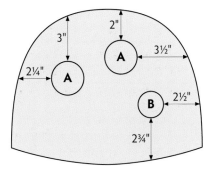

Appliqué placement guide

4. Mark a dashed circle ¼" *inside* the solid lines you traced. Cut along the dashed lines, and then clip around the circles toward the solid lines.

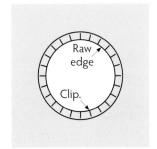

5. Turn the clipped edges of the circles under (to the wrong side) and press. You can skip this step if you prefer and simply turn the edges under as you hand stitch the appliqués.

6. With right sides facing up, center one 4" fabric square behind each circle on the tea-cozy exterior and pin in place. Hand or machine baste ½" outside the solid line of the circle and remove the pins.

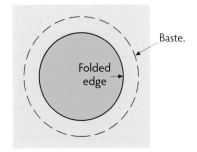

7. Using an embroidery hoop, if desired, and thread to match the linen, hand stitch the linen to the print fabric using a tiny overcast stitch or a slip stitch. If you didn't press the clipped edges under, turn them under as you sew.

Embroidery-Hoop Help

Amy finds it helpful to use an embroidery hoop while hand stitching the appliqué. She prefers to then remove the hoop and sew the embroidered stitches without it—especially the running stitch. Experiment and do whatever feels most comfortable for you.

Embroidering the Tea Cozy

1. Using a running stitch and embroidery floss in a color that matches each reverse-appliquéd circle, stitch about ⅛" from the turned edge around each circle. Use an embroidery hoop if desired. Trim excess fabric from the 4" squares, leaving about ½" beyond the stitching.

2. With a removable marking pen or chalk, draw the stem and leaves onto the right side of the tea cozy below the circles.

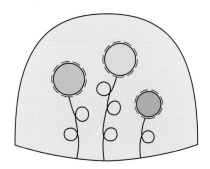

Embroidery placement guide

3. Using a backstitch and light-green embroidery floss, embroider along the traced lines. Start at the top and end about ¼" from the lower raw edge.

Backstitch

Making the Tea Cozy

1. To make the tab, fold the 3" x 5" rectangle of orange fabric in half lengthwise, wrong sides together, and press. Open and fold each long side in, again with wrong sides together, so the raw edges meet at the center crease. Press. Fold in half along the original crease and press a final time. You'll have a ¾" x 5" strip. Topstitch close to each long edge.

Center fold

2. Place the front and back linen pieces, right sides together and raw edges aligned. Fold the tab from step 1 in half so the raw edges align. Place the tab between the front and back exterior pieces at the center top so that the folded edge of the tab is inside and the raw edges align with the raw edges of the linen. Pin in place along all raw edges except the bottom and sew together along the sides and top using a ½" seam allowance. Stitch back and forth an extra time at the tab to attach it securely.

3. Notch the seam allowance along the curves and turn the cozy right side out.

4. Make a quilt sandwich of the teal lining and Insul-Bright by stacking them in the following order: Insul-Bright, tea-cozy lining (right side up), tea-cozy lining (wrong side up), Insul-Bright. Align raw edges and pin in place along all edges except the bottom.

5. Using a ⅝" seam allowance and a walking foot, sew the sandwich together through all four layers. If you don't have a walking foot, sew slowly and carefully, holding the layers of fabric together so they don't slip.

6. Trim the seam allowance to ¼" and clip along the curves. Do not turn right side out, but open into a dome or upside-down bowl shape by separating the lining fabrics from each other.

7. Place the tea-cozy lining you just sewed inside the tea-cozy exterior so that the Insul-Bright is facing the wrong side of the linen. When you look inside, you should see the right sides of the lining fabric. Align all raw edges along the bottom and pin them in place.

8. To make the binding strip, fold one short end of the gray print 3" x 42" strip in ½" toward the wrong side and press. Then fold in half lengthwise, wrong sides together, and press again.

9. On the inside (lining side) of the tea cozy, and starting in the back of the tea cozy and with the folded short end of the binding strip, align the raw edges of the binding strip with the raw edges of the tea-cozy bottom. Pin in place and carefully work your way around the inside of the tea cozy with the binding strip, removing and replacing pins as you go. When you get to the end of the binding strip, trim the excess strip and tuck the raw edge end inside the folded end. Sew ⅜" from the raw edge all around to secure the binding.

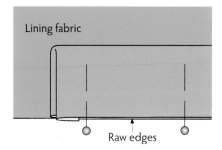

Lining fabric

Raw edges

10. Fold the binding to the outside of the tea cozy and pin in place so that it just covers the line of stitching. Using a zigzag stitch and thread to match, topstitch along the folded edge of the binding to secure.

place mats

Designed and made by Amy Struckmeyer.
Finished size: 12" x 17"

Materials for 4 Place Mats

Yardage is based on 42"-wide fabric.

⅞ yard of natural linen (or cotton) for fronts
⅞ yard of gray print for backs
⅛ yard of teal print for appliqué
⅛ yard of orange print for appliqué
⅛ yard of yellow print for appliqué
2 yards of 20"-wide lightweight fusible interfacing
Embroidery floss in teal, orange, yellow, and
    light green
Needles for embroidery and hand sewing
6" embroidery hoop (optional)
Spray starch or starch alternative (optional)
Cardstock

Cutting

From the linen, cut:
4 rectangles, 13" x 18"

From the gray print, cut:
4 rectangles, 13" x 18"

From *each* of the teal, orange, and yellow prints, cut:
4 squares, 4" x 4" (12 total)

From the interfacing, cut:
12 squares, 3¾" x 3¾"
4 rectangles, 12½" x 17½"

Applying the Reverse Appliqué

1. Center and fuse one 3¾" square of fusible interfacing to the wrong side of each of the 12 print 4" squares.

2. Starch and press the place-mat front pieces. This is helpful for holding the shape of the fabric while stitching the appliqué.

3. To round the corners, find a circular object that's about 5" diameter. Amy used a small saucer. Place this at each corner of one place-mat front and trace the shape; then cut along your marked lines to round each corner. Use this first place-mat front as a pattern to round the corners of the three remaining place-mat fronts.

4. Make templates from cardstock using the circle patterns on page 51. On each place-mat front, trace two A circles and one B circle. You can place these in the same location to make each place mat the same or mix them up to make each place mat a little different, as Amy did. She placed all of the circles toward the outer edges so they will still be at least partially visible with a table setting placed on top. Allow enough room for a ½" seam allowance plus at least 1" along the edges. Mark a dashed circle ¼" *inside* the solid lines you traced. Cut along the dashed lines, and then clip around the circles toward the solid lines.

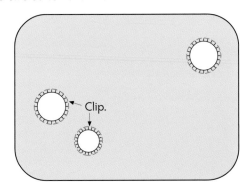

5. Turn the clipped edges of the circles under (to the fabric wrong side) and press. You can skip this step if you prefer and turn the edges under as you hand stitch the appliqué.

6. With right sides facing up, center one 4" fabric square behind each cutout circle and pin in place. Hand or machine baste ½" from the solid line of the circle.

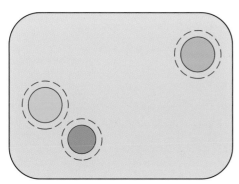

7. Using an embroidery hoop, if desired, and thread to match the linen, hand stitch the linen to the print using a tiny overcast stitch or a slip stitch. If you did not press the clipped edges of the circle under, turn them under now as you sew.

8. Using a running stitch and embroidery floss in a color that matches each circle, stitch about ⅛" from the turned edge around each circle. Use an embroidery hoop if desired. Trim the excess fabric from the 4" squares, leaving about ½" beyond the stitching.

Assembling the Place Mats

1. Using a place-mat front as a pattern, place it over the place-mat back and trim the excess fabric at the corners of the back. Repeat for each place mat.

2. Center a rectangle of interfacing on the wrong side of one place-mat back and trim the corners along each curve approximately ¼" smaller than the fabric. Fuse the interfacing to the wrong side of the back. Repeat with the remaining three place-mat backs.

3. Position one place-mat front on one place-mat back, right sides together and raw edges aligned. Pin in place and stitch around the edges using a ½" seam allowance and leaving a 5" opening for turning along one short end. Repeat with the remaining three place mats.

4. Notch each curved corner within the seam allowance. Then turn right side out and press. Slip-stitch the opening closed.

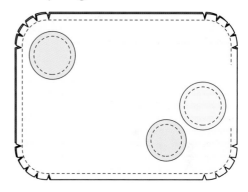

5. Topstitch all around each place mat ¼" from the edge.

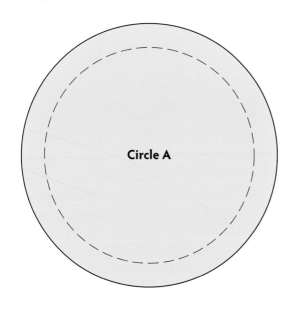

Circle A

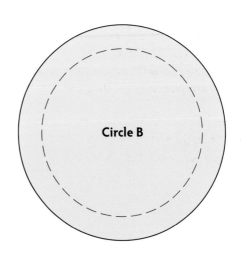

Circle B

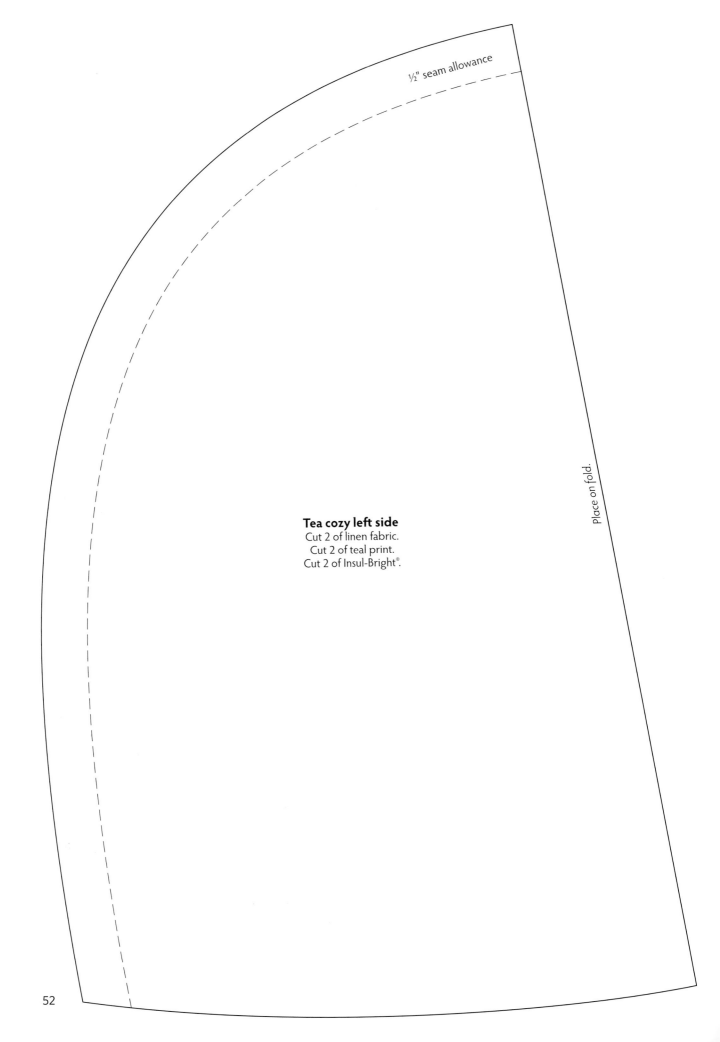

½" seam allowance

Tea cozy left side
Cut 2 of linen fabric.
Cut 2 of teal print.
Cut 2 of Insul-Bright®.

Place on fold.

garden party tablecloth and napkins

V intage linens and tablecloths are widely sought after, but many have small stains or holes, mended tears, or are just too small for modern dining tables. Make the most of lovely yet slightly imperfect vintage linens by salvaging the best parts of one or two to use in this modern and useful project. Try to find cloths that are large enough so you can cut 9" square blocks from them using the best designs on the cloth. Coordinating cloth napkins, edged in rickrack, add extra charm to your table!

tablecloth

Designed and pieced by Kari Ramsay. Quilted by Tony and Carolyn Ratola.

Finished size: 75½" x 75½"

Materials

Yardage is based on 42"-wide fabric.

1 vintage tablecloth (or more as needed)

2¼ yards of small-scale blue floral for medallion border and outer border

1⅝ yards of pink dot for setting triangles and appliquéd block backgrounds

1½ yards of red gingham* for inner border, Dresden wedges, and Orange Peel appliqués

1⅓ yards of light-blue polka dot for Dresden center, medallion background, and Orange Peel background

⅝ yard of blue print for Dresden wedges and yo-yos

¾ yard of red stripe for bias binding

5 yards of fabric for backing

7½ yards of white rickrack, 1½" wide

84" x 84" piece of batting

Template plastic or freezer paper for templates

Optional: Clover Yo-Yo Maker, extra large

The gingham used in the tablecloth shown was printed on the bias.

Choosing Your Vintage Tablecloth

Vintage linens often have imperfections such as tiny pinholes, storage yellowing, or stains. Often you can cut around these—in fact, on some online selling sites these linens are referred to as "cutter" tablecloths. Inspect your cloth to find any pinholes or staining so you can avoid those areas as much as possible. Fussy cutting these squares is a fun way to focus on the beauty of the prints in vintage cloths.

Cutting

Make templates from template plastic or freezer paper for the Dresden wedges, Orange Peel shapes, and circle using the patterns on pages 59 and 60.

From the blue print, cut:

4 squares, 6" x 6"

8 large wedges

4 small wedges

From the red gingham, cut *on the lengthwise grain:*

4 strips, 2½" x 50"

8 large wedges

8 small wedges

16 orange peels

Continued on page 55

Continued from page 53

From the pink dot, cut:

1 square, 24½" x 24½"

4 squares, 4¾" x 4¾"

4 squares, 13⅜" x 13⅜"; cut into quarters diagonally
to yield 16 setting triangles

2 squares, 7" x 7"; cut in half diagonally to yield 4
corner setting triangles

From the light-blue polka dot, cut:

2 squares, 17⅞" x 17⅞"; cut in half diagonally to yield
4 triangles

4 squares, 9" x 9"

1 circle

From the small-scale blue floral, cut *on the length-wise grain*:

4 strips, 6" x 81"

4 strips, 4¾" x 34½"

From the vintage tablecloth(s), cut:

12 squares, 9" x 9"

From the red stripe, cut:

2½"-wide bias strips to total 320"

Making the Dresden Blocks

All seam allowances are ¼".

1. Make the large blue Dresden wedges by folding
   each wedge in half vertically, right sides together.
   Pin the fold of the fabric together and sew along
   the top raw edges. Turn the wedge right side out,
   finger-pressing the seam to one side. Poke the
   point out fully with a blunt bamboo skewer. It has
   now become a petal. Repeat for the remaining
   blue and red large wedges to make eight of each.

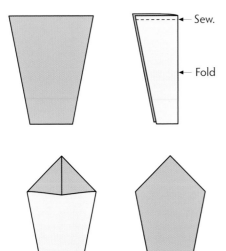

2. Lay out the Dresden petals in a circle, alternating
   the blue and red fabrics. Pin and sew eight of the
   petals together along the long raw edges, right
   sides together. Press the seam allowances to one
   side. Repeat with the other eight petals. This will
   give you two halves of a Dresden plate.

3. With right sides together, pin and sew the two
   halves of the Dresden plate together. Press the
   Dresden plate.

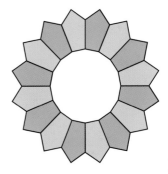

4. Fold the pink dot 24½" background square in half
   horizontally and then in half vertically. Finger-
   press along the folds to mark the center of the
   square.

5. Lay the Dresden plate unit on top of the square
   and line up one seam with each crease.

Measure from the center of the square to each side of the plate to ensure the plate is centered on the square. Pin in place and appliqué by hand or machine.

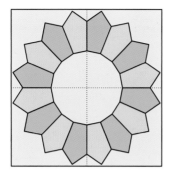

6. Turn under the raw edges of the light-blue polka-dot circle ¼" all around. Press the edges. Center the circle on the Dresden plate. Hand or machine appliqué the circle in place.

7. Repeat step 1 on page 55 to make eight red and four blue small Dresden petals.

8. Pin and sew, right sides together, one blue petal between two red petals to create a fan. Press the seam allowances to one side. Make four.

Make 4.

9. Lay one fan right side up in the corner of a pink 4¾" square. Align the edges of the fan with the edges of the square. Pin and appliqué the fan in place by hand or machine. Make four fan blocks.

Make 4.

Making the Orange Peel Blocks

The Orange Peel blocks in the tablecloth shown were made using raw-edge appliqué. You can leave the edges raw as Kari did, or turn them under ¼".

1. Place four Orange Peels on a light-blue 9" square as shown. Pin in place and appliqué by hand or machine. For raw edges, sew ¼" from the edge of each peel.

2. Repeat step 1 to make four blocks.

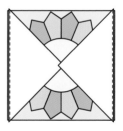

Make 4.

Assembling the Tablecloth

1. Sew light-blue triangles to opposite sides of the Dresden plate block. Press the seam allowances toward the triangles. Sew the remaining two triangles to the square and press.

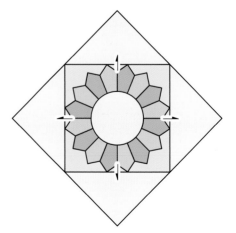

2. Sew a fan block to each end of two blue floral 4¾" x 34½" strips. The fan corners should point toward each other on each end of the strip. Press the seam allowances toward the blue strips.

Make 2.

3. Pin and sew the blue floral 4¾" x 34½" strips to opposite sides of the center square from step 1. Press the seam allowances away from the center square. Add the strips with fan blocks on each end and press.

4. To create the pieced setting triangles for the corners of the tablecloth, you'll need three 9" tablecloth squares, one Orange Peel block, four pink 13⅜" triangles, and one pink 7" triangle. Arrange the blocks and triangles as shown and sew them into rows, aligning the right angles of the side triangles with the blocks. Sew the rows together and add the corner triangle last. Press the seam allowances as indicated by arrows. Make four large pieced triangles.

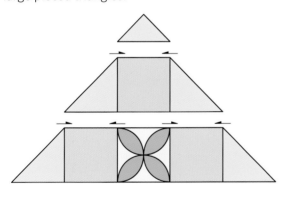

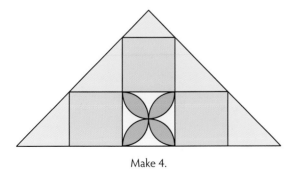

Make 4.

5. Center the pieced triangles along opposite sides of the center medallion unit. Place them right sides together, pin, and sew in place. Add pieced

triangles to the remaining sides. Press the seam allowances toward the tablecloth center.

6. Measure the tablecloth top through the center horizontally. Cut two of the red gingham strips to that measurement. Sew a strip to each side of the tablecloth and press the seam allowances toward the inner border.

7. Measure the tablecloth top through the center vertically, including the borders just added. Cut two red gingham strips to that measurement. Pin and sew them to the top and bottom of the tablecloth.

8. Repeat the steps to measure, cut, and sew the blue floral strips to the tablecloth.

9. Add the jumbo rickrack to the tablecloth by pinning and sewing it along the inside edge of the inner border. You can add the rickrack after the tablecloth has been quilted if you prefer.

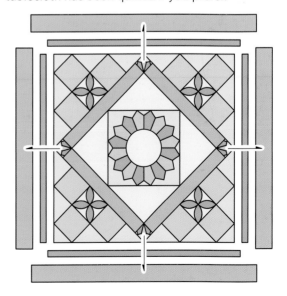

10. Make and attach binding using the red-striped bias strips. Add a label.

Adding the Yo-Yos

The yo-yos are an optional embellishment for the center of the Orange Peel blocks. Use the four blue-print 6" squares and refer to the instructions included with the yo-yo maker to make the yo-yos.

If you don't have a yo-yo maker, do this instead. Make a circle template that's 5" in diameter. Trace it on the right side of the blue-print squares. Cut the circle out ¼" from the line. Turn the ¼" to the wrong side and sew with a running stitch around the circle. Draw up the stitches to gather the circle and fasten off with a few backstitches. If the opening in the center is too big, take the stitches out and make them longer.

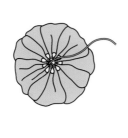

Hand stitch the yo-yos to the tablecloth after the quilting is complete.

napkins

Designed and made by Kari Ramsay.
Finished size: 12" x 12"

Materials for 4 Napkins

Yardage is based on 42"-wide fabric.

1¼ yards of pink floral
4¾ yards of white ⅝" rickrack

Cutting

The circle pattern is on page 60.

From the pink floral, cut:
8 circles

From the rickrack, cut:
4 pieces, 41" long

Sewing the Napkins

1. Draw a sewing line ¼" from the raw edges on the right side of one pink circle. Center and pin a length of rickrack on the sewing line. Place pins approximately 1" apart to keep the rickrack from shifting as you sew. Leave the tails of rickrack extending out about 1½" at each end where they meet.

2. Place a second pink circle on top of the first one, right sides together, aligning the raw edges. Pin the circles together.

3. Sew around the circle using a ¼" seam allowance; leave a 3" opening where the tails of rickrack are. Clip around the raw edges and turn the circle right side out. Press.

4. Press under the edges of the opening ¼" and tuck the rickrack tails inside the opening, trimming as needed. The ends of both sides of the rickrack should meet up perfectly where they're tucked into the circle.

5. Topstitch ⅛" from the edge of the circle. Press.

6. Repeat steps 1–5 for the remaining three napkins.

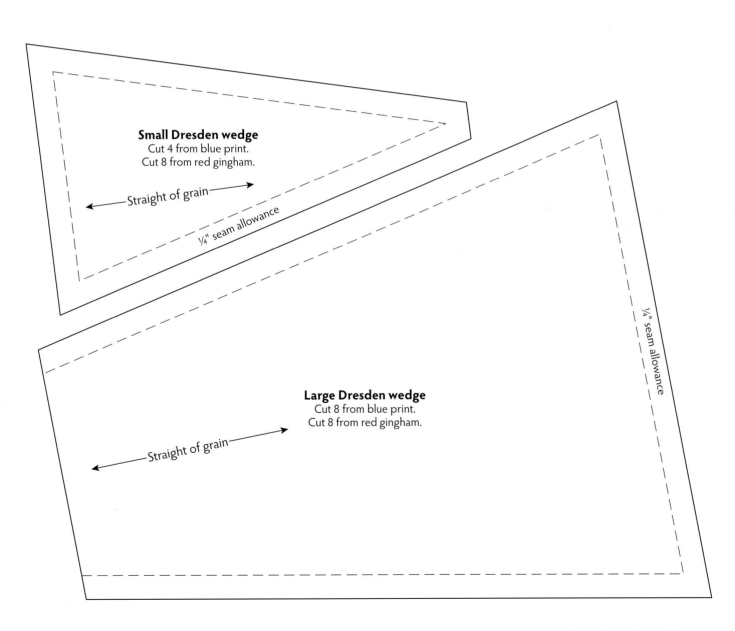

Small Dresden wedge
Cut 4 from blue print.
Cut 8 from red gingham.

Straight of grain

¼" seam allowance

Large Dresden wedge
Cut 8 from blue print.
Cut 8 from red gingham.

Straight of grain

¼" seam allowance

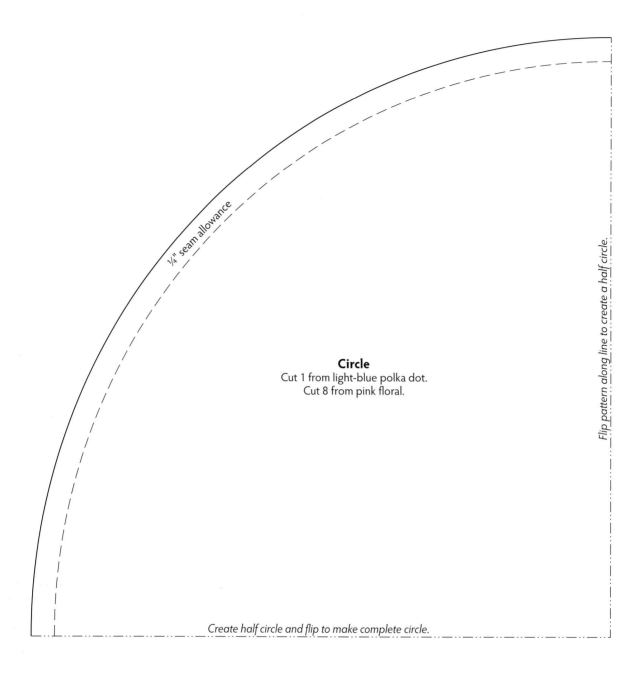

¼" seam allowance

Circle
Cut 1 from light-blue polka dot.
Cut 8 from pink floral.

Flip pattern along line to create a half circle.

Create half circle and flip to make complete circle.

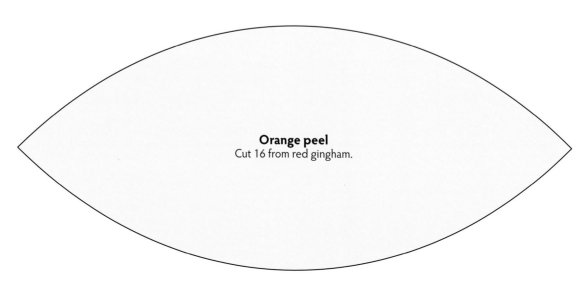

Orange peel
Cut 16 from red gingham.

bistro tablecloth and napkins

*E*veryone needs a go-to tablecloth and napkin set that works well with anything. This black-and-white bistro set is sure to be just the thing to add flair to any meal while still being super practical. It's the perfect size to be a table topper on the center of your formal dining table or to fit just right on a kitchenette table. And all it takes is some simple appliqué to add modern style to a basic tablecloth.

Designed and made by Melissa Corry.
Finished tablecloth size: 41" x 41"
Finished napkin size: 9" x 9"

Materials for 1 Tablecloth and 4 Napkins

Yardage is based on 42"-wide fabric.

1½ yards of white solid for tablecloth and napkins
⅝ yard of black solid for appliqués
1 yard of 18"-wide fusible web

Cutting

From the white solid, cut:
1 square, 42" x 42"
4 squares, 10" x 10"

Sewing the Tablecloth and Napkins

1. Fold under one raw edge of the large white square ¼" to wrong side and press. Fold under ¼" again and press.

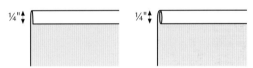

2. Repeat for each side, taking care to keep the corners flat and square.

3. On the wrong side of the fabric, sew ¼" from the edge along one side of the square to secure the fold. Backstitch at the beginning and end. Repeat for each side of the square to finish the hem around the tablecloth.

Stitch.

4. Repeat steps 1–3 for each of the four small white squares to make the napkins.

Adding Appliqué

1. Using the patterns on pages 64–66, cut letters and prepare the shapes for the words *SOUP, SALAD, BREAD,* and *DESSERT*. Also cut and prepare four knives, four spoons, and eight forks.

2. Arrange the appliqués on the tablecloth as shown, placing the words ½" from the edge and centering them on each side. Place a knife in each corner, with the end of the handles 2½" from the corners. Forks and spoons are approximately 1" away from each side of the knives. Fuse in place following the manufacturer's instructions for the fusible web.

3. Arrange the fork on the napkins as shown and fuse in place.

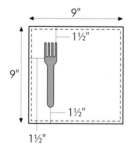

4. Stitch around each appliqué with a blanket stitch by hand or machine.

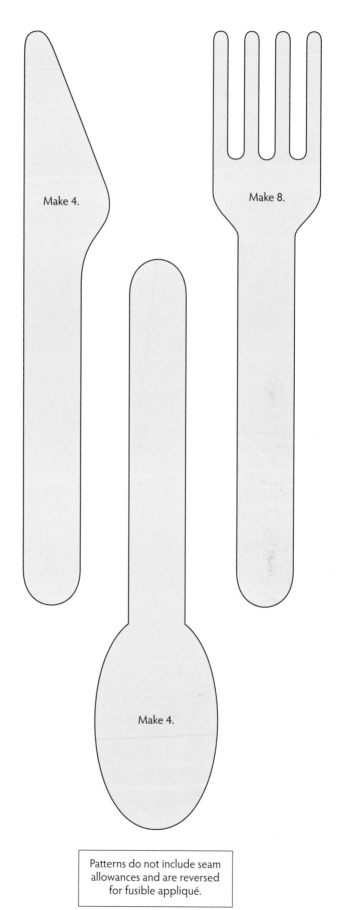

Make 4.

Make 8.

Make 4.

Patterns do not include seam allowances and are reversed for fusible appliqué.

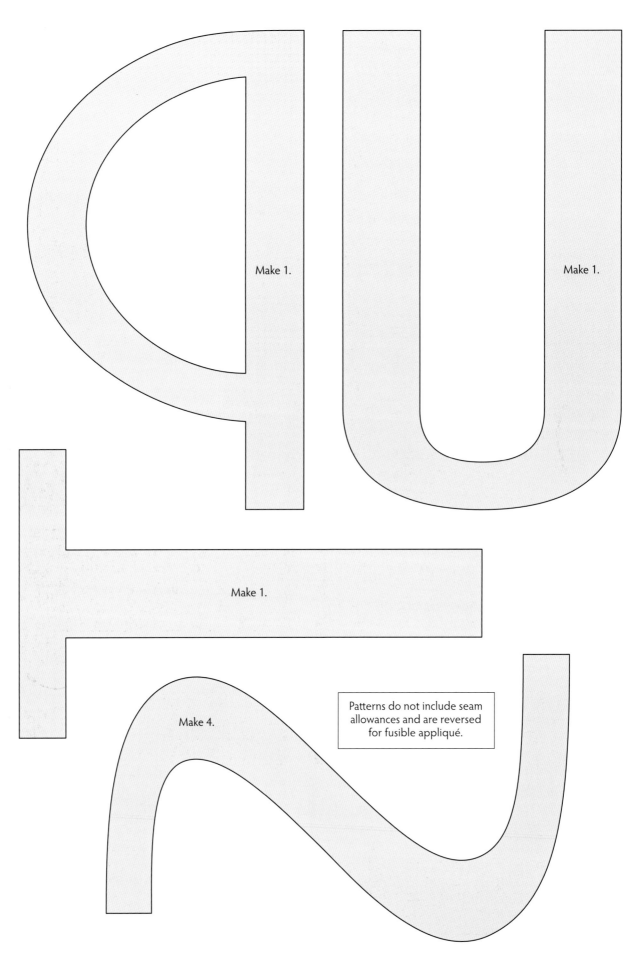

Make 1.

Make 1.

Make 1.

Make 4.

Patterns do not include seam
allowances and are reversed
for fusible appliqué.

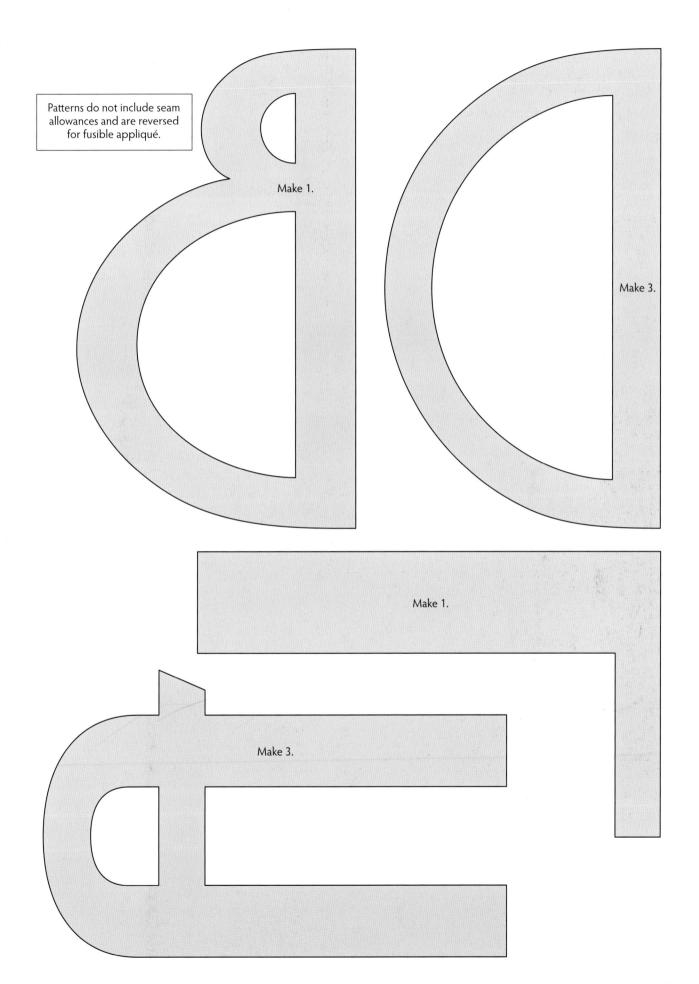

Patterns do not include seam allowances and are reversed for fusible appliqué.

Make 1.

Make 3.

Make 1.

Make 3.

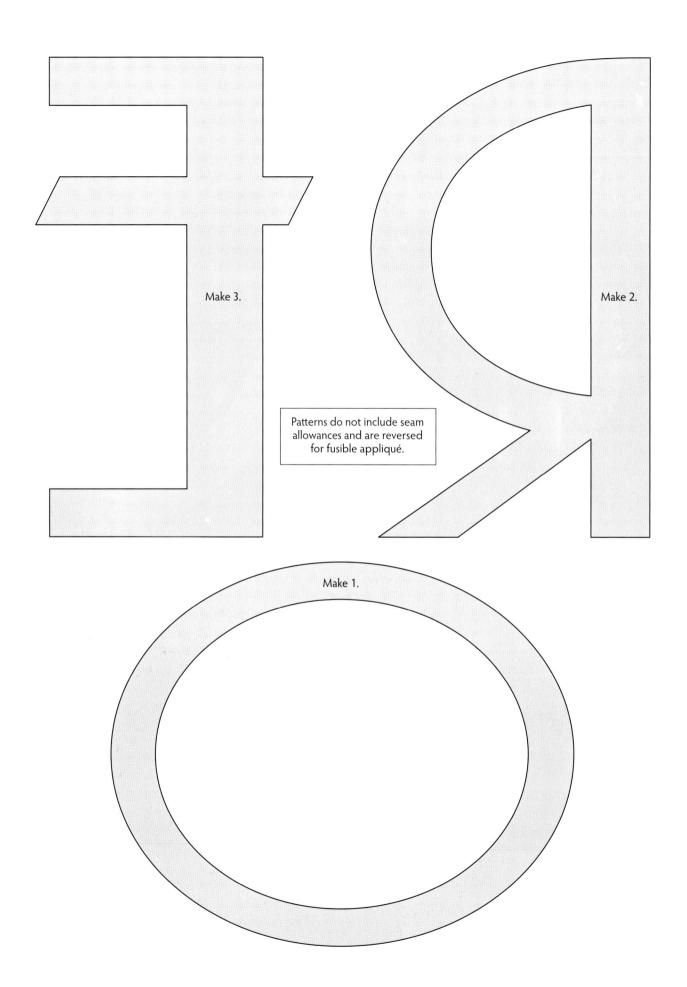

Make 3.

Make 2.

Patterns do not include seam
allowances and are reversed
for fusible appliqué.

Make 1.

shattered strips table runner and place mats

Great for scraps! Improvisational patchwork and a quilt-as-you-go technique join forces to make these pretty place mats and table runner. Make them as quick-and-easy gifts or to add some pizzazz to your own dining area.

table runner

Designed and made by Missy Shepler.
Finished size: 10" x 40"

Materials

Yardage is based on 42"-wide fabric.

1½ yards *total* of scraps in assorted colors for runner
⅝ yard of dark-gray solid for backing and binding
12" x 42" piece of batting

Cutting

From the dark-gray solid, cut:
1 rectangle, 12" x 42"
3 strips, 2¼" x 42"

From the scraps, cut:
50 to 60 strips, 1" to 3" wide x 15" long

Assembling the Table Runner

1. Place the dark-gray backing wrong side up and layer the batting on top, smoothing it in place to make sure that there are no wrinkles. Pin baste with safety pins to keep the layers together.

2. Decide on your color plan and sort your fabric strips. The table runner shown is loosely based on the color wheel, creating a rainbow of colors from red to orange, yellow, green, blue-green, and blue.

3. Beginning at one short edge, place the first strip right side up on the batting and pin it in place at the top and bottom. Audition a second strip, visualizing the angle of your stitching line. Flip this second strip over along the planned stitching line

so that the strips are right sides together. Stitch the strips together, sewing through the batting and all layers of fabric and stitching ¼" from the raw edge of the second strip.

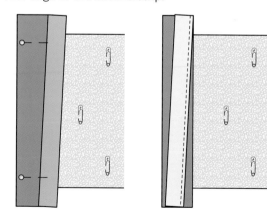

4. Flip the second strip right side up and check the piecing. If all looks good, trim the seam allowances to ¼" and press the strip open. Trim the edges even with the batting.

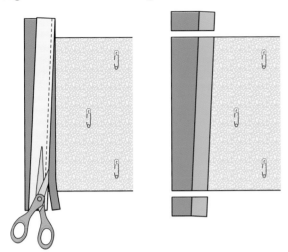

5. Select a third strip, audition, and sew in the same manner. Continue adding pieces until the batting is covered.

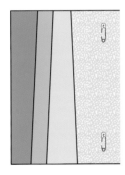

6. Add any additional quilting, if desired.

7. Using a rotary ruler and fabric marker, measure and mark a 10" x 40" rectangle to indicate the outer edges of the runner. Sew a scant ¼" seam through all layers inside the marked line. Trim the excess fabric and batting along the marked lines.

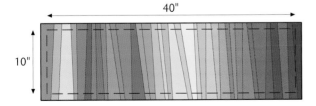

Finishing

1. Make and attach binding using the dark-gray strips.

2. Add a label if desired.

place mats

Designed and made by Missy Shepler.
Finished size: 12" x 18"

Materials for 4 Place Mats

Yardage is based on 42"-wide fabric.

⅝ yard *total* of assorted green prints
⅝ yard *total* of assorted blue prints
⅝ yard *total* of assorted red prints
⅝ yard *total* of assorted yellow to orange prints
1⅞ yards of dark-gray solid for silverware pocket, backing, and binding
28" x 40" piece of batting

Cutting

From the dark-gray solid, cut:
4 rectangles, 4" x 24"
4 rectangles, 14" x 20"
7 strips, 2¼" x 42"

From *each color* of the assorted scraps, cut:
12 to 20 strips, 1" to 3" wide x 17" long

From the batting, cut:
4 rectangles, 14" x 20"

Assembling the Place Mat

1. Place a dark-gray 14" x 20" rectangle wrong side up and layer the batting on top, smoothing it in place to make sure that there are no wrinkles. Pin baste with safety pins to keep the layers together.

2. Beginning at the left edge of the place mat and working with your chosen color, follow steps 3–5 for the table runner beginning on page 67 or, see "Changing Directions" on page 71 for options. Continue adding pieces until you've covered 16" to 17" of the place-mat width.

3. Using a rotary ruler and fabric marker, measure and mark a 12" x 18" rectangle to indicate the outer edges of the place mat. Sew a scant ¼" seam through all layers inside the marked line. Trim the excess fabric and batting along the marked lines.

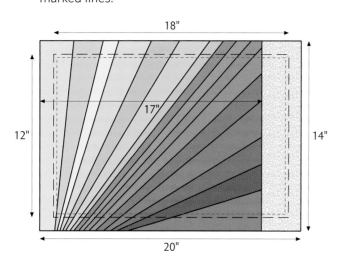

4. With right sides together, fold a dark-gray 4" x 24" silverware pocket in half so that it measures 4" x 12" and press. Fold the short edge of the top layer of fabric down to meet the fold, revealing the right side of the fabric, and press again.

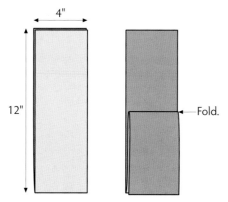

5. Place the folded silverware pocket right side up on the short right side of the place mat, making sure that the left edge overlaps the piecing by at least ¼". Flip the silverware pocket wrong side up to the left. Measure 3½" from the right edge and pin the pocket in place. Stitch the pocket edge in place ¼" from the raw edge. Check the piecing, trim the seam allowance of the strip to ¼", flip the pocket to the right side, and press.

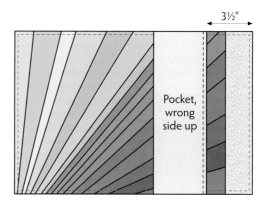

6. Stitch a scant ¼" from the edges of the place mat to secure the pocket.

7. Add additional quilting to the area above the pocket and to the strips on the left, if desired.

8. Make and attach the binding using the dark-gray strips.

Quilting the Pocket

In the place mats shown here, the top areas of the silverware pocket were meander quilted, making it easier to insert the silverware.

Changing Directions

Don't limit yourself to single-direction straight-line stitching. Experiment with stitching lines that radiate from one direction (sunburst), multidirectional lines (splintered glass), wavy lines (ocean waves), and surrounded squares (scattered squares). The same basic technique of auditioning and adding strips is used in each design.

For a sunburst design, position and sew strips to suggest rays of light originating from a single source. Avoid making all seams converge on a single spot, however, as too many seam allowances in one space add unnecessary bulk to the place mat.

Multidirectional lines, as in the splintered-glass design, are achieved by adding a partial strip to a full strip, and then overlapping both strips with a third piece. This requires a bit of preplanning to avoid extra fabric layers beneath the covering strip.

Make wavy line designs by sewing gentle curves with bias-cut strips. Cutting fabric on the bias, rather than the straight grain, allows the fabric to stretch just a bit. Narrow strips work better than wide sections for waves. Be sure to keep curves smooth and subtle—no tight turns!—and take extra care when pressing.

Scattered squares are made in a similar manner as traditional Log Cabin blocks. Start with a center square—or square-ish shape—and then add rectangular strips to each edge. Wedge-shaped strips distort the square and add visual interest to the design.

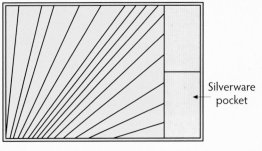

Silverware pocket

Sunburst

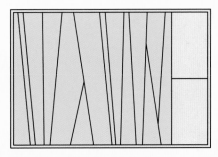

Splintered glass

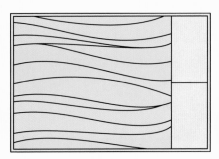

Ocean waves

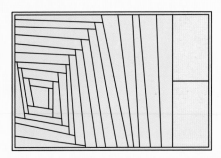

Scattered squares

cartwheels table runner and napkins

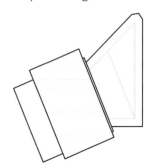

*T*his cheerful table runner and matching napkin set adds a personal touch to any tabletop. Simple paper piecing creates perfect points without the use of pins. In addition to the rolling "wheels," the blocks create two very different spinning designs—inside the wheels and also at the block intersections.

table runner

Designed and made by Amy Ellis.
Fabric is Boho by Urban Chiks for Moda.
Finished size: 12½" x 60½"
Finished block: 6" x 6"

Materials

Yardage is based on 42"-wide fabric. Fat eighths measure 9" x 21".

1 yard of white solid for blocks
⅞ yard of blue print for blocks
20 fat eighths or 20 squares, 10" x 10", for blocks
⅜ yard of multicolored print for binding
1¼ yards of fabric for backing
18" x 66" piece of batting

Cutting

From the blue print, cut:
8 strips, 3" x 42"; crosscut into 160 rectangles,
    3" x 1¾"

From the white solid, cut:
5 strips, 2½" x 42"; crosscut into 80 squares,
    2½" x 2½"
4 strips, 4" x 42"; crosscut into 80 rectangles, 2" x 4"

From *each* of the 20 fat eighths or 10" squares, cut:
4 squares, 2½" x 2½" (80 total)
4 rectangles, 2" x 4" (80 total)

From the multicolored print, cut:
4 strips, 2¼" x 42"

Assembling the Blocks

Before you begin piecing, shorten the stitch length on your sewing machine to 1.5 mm (16 or 17 stitches per inch). This will perforate the papers as you sew, making fast work of removing them later. The paper pattern acts as a guide, indicating where to sew and where to trim. To understand the paper-piecing process better, remember that the paper lies on the *wrong* side of the block; once the paper is removed, the wrong side of the fabric will be visible.

1. Copy 80 of each of the quarter-block foundation patterns on page 76 using a photocopier (you can fit four patterns on each page). Cut each pattern piece away from the others.

2. First make the A pattern pieces. Place a white 2½" square right side up on the wrong side of the paper pattern, covering the area labeled 1. With right sides together, add a blue rectangle on top, making sure that the seam line is covered by ¼". Hold the piece up to the light to check.

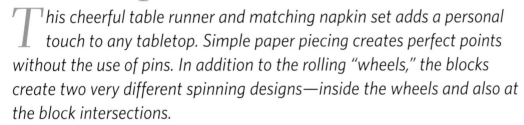

3. Flip the pieces over so the paper foundation is on top. Sew directly on the marked line between pieces 1 and 2 through the paper and fabrics. Begin and end the stitching beyond the block perimeter; the area outside the dashed line will be

73

trimmed away later. From the fabric side, fold the blue strip into position over area 2 and press the seam.

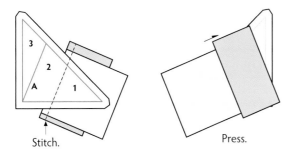

Stitch.

Press.

4. Add a rectangle cut from the fat eighths to the foundation in the same way. Then press and trim the units along the dashed cutting line.

Trim.

5. Continue to piece the triangles until you have made four A triangles. Make four B triangles, beginning each with a fat-eighth rectangle and ending with a white square.

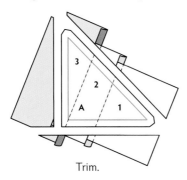

Make 4 of each.

6. Sew an A and a B triangle together to make a quarter-block. Press the seam allowances in one direction. Make four quarter-blocks.

Make 4.

7. Before joining the quarter-blocks, tear away the paper in the seam allowances at the center; this will make it less bulky and easier for your machine to sew. Sew the quarter-blocks into halves and press the seam allowances in the same direction as the other seams. Sew the block halves together to complete the block.

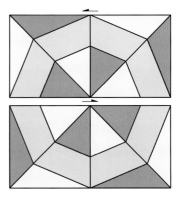

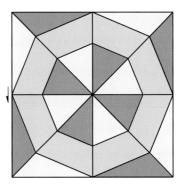

8. Repeat steps 2–7 to make a total of 20 blocks.

Paper-Piecing Tips

- Shorten your stitch length to 1.5 mm (16 or 17 stitches per inch) to easily remove papers.

- The paper pattern will be on the *wrong* side of the block. Make sure your fabrics are all facing right side out once pressed over the seam allowances.

- Hold the paper up to the light to verify that you have enough seam allowance.

- Copy an extra paper pattern or two; use these for practice before you start.

- Depending on how you like to sew, you can repeat the same step for each block, or complete one block before starting the next.

Assembling the Table Runner

1. Arrange the blocks in two rows of 10 blocks each. Sew the blocks together in rows, pressing the seam allowances in alternating directions. Sew the rows together. Press the seam allowances in the same direction.

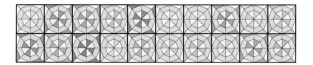

2. Before removing the paper, stay stitch ⅛" from the edges; this will prevent any seams from opening while removing the paper.

3. Remove the papers from the quilt top and press.

4. Layer the table-runner top, batting, and backing; baste the layers together. Quilt as desired. Amy quilted wavy stitches around the center ring in each block, and then added a little hand quilting to the centers. Be creative and enjoy showing off your handiwork!

5. Make and attach the binding using the multi-colored strips. Add a label if desired.

napkins

Designed and made by Amy Ellis.
Finished size: 20" x 20"

Materials for 6 Napkins

1 set of 6 cotton napkins, 20" x 20"
¼ yard of white solid
¼ yard of blue print
6 squares, 10" x 10", of assorted prints*
¼ yard of 18"-wide lightweight fusible web

6 charm squares, 5" x 5", are also an option.

Cutting

From the white solid, cut:
2 strips, 2" x 42"; crosscut into 24 squares, 2" x 2"

From the blue print, cut:
2 strips, 2½" x 42"; crosscut into 48 rectangles, 1½" x 2½"

From *each of the 6* prints, cut:
4 squares, 2" x 2" (24 total)

Making the Blocks

1. Make 48 copies of the triangle foundation pattern C below using a photocopier (you can fit six to eight patterns on each page).

2. Paper piece the triangles in the same manner as for the table-runner blocks, following steps 2 and 3 beginning on page 73. Make four triangles starting with a white square and four starting with a print square.

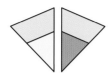

Make 4 of each.

3. Sew the eight triangles together to make the block, removing paper in the seam allowances as needed. Make six octagonal blocks.

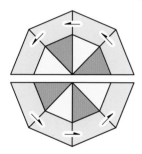 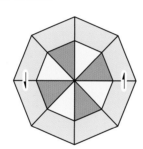

Make 6.

4. Remove the paper and trim any little triangles of fabric (sometimes called "dog-ears") that extend beyond the edge of the block.

Appliquéing the Napkins

1. Place one of the blocks on the paper side of the fusible web and trace around it six times. Cut out the fusible-web shapes about ¼" *inside* the traced lines.

2. Following the manufacturer's instructions, apply the fusible web to the wrong side of each completed block. Then fuse the blocks to one corner of the napkins, keeping the design ¼" from any existing seams.

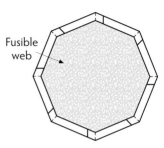

Fusible web

3. Use a blanket or zigzag stitch to appliqué the blocks to the napkin. The combination of fusing and stitching makes them ready for company and the washing machine time and again.

Table runner

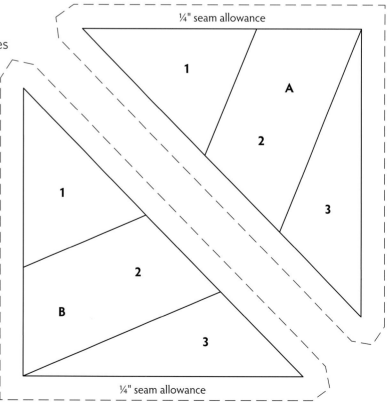

Make 80 of each for table runner.

Napkin

¼" seam allowance

Make 8 for each napkin.

add a little spice

embroidery-hoop memo minders

*C*olorful embroidery hoops create the frames for these multipurpose bulletin boards. Use them to organize notes to yourself, the kids' schedules, family photos, or your grocery list.

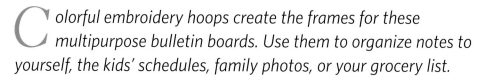

Designed and made by Linda Turner Griepentrog.
Fabrics by Timeless Treasures. Embroidery hoops from Coats and Clark.
Finished size: 10" diameter

Materials for 4 Memo Minders

Yardage is based on 42"-wide fabric unless otherwise noted.

⅜ yard *each* of 3 coordinating kitchen prints
⅜ yard of chalkboard fabric (or 1 square, 13" x 13")
⅜ yard of 45"-wide fusible fleece
¼ yard of 20"-wide fusible interfacing
4 plastic embroidery hoops, 10" diameter
2½ yards of grosgrain ribbon, ⅝" wide, for basic and photo boards
1 yard of grosgrain ribbon, ⅝" wide, for pocketed board and chalkboard
3 buttons, ½" diameter
12" x 12" piece of foam board, ¼" thick
Fabric glue
Chalk holder and chalk
Craft knife

Cutting and Preparation

1. Trace the perimeter of the inner hoop onto fusible fleece and cut out three circles. Following the manufacturer's instructions, fuse the fleece circle to the wrong side of each of the three print fabrics. Draw a line 1" away around the fleece circle and cut out the circle on the drawn line.

2. For the pocketed version, cut a second fabric circle the same size as the fleece-backed circle; cut a half circle that same diameter from interfacing.

3. For the chalkboard, trace around the perimeter of the inner hoop on the wrong side of chalkboard fabric. Add 1" around the drawn circle and cut out the circle on the drawn line.

4. Trace around the perimeter of the inner hoop onto the foam board. Cut out the circle using a craft knife. It's important that the foam circle does not overhang the hoop edge; trim if needed. It should be the size of the *outside* of the inner hoop, not the inside of it (so it won't fit inside the hoop).

Assembling the Basic Board

1. Apply glue to the front surface of the inner hoop. Center the fleece-backed fabric over the hoop and finger-press in place to adhere.

2. Loosen the outer hoop adjustment screw enough to push the hoop over the inner hoop, noting any directional fabric orientation to the upper hoop. Push the outer hoop over the inner hoop and tighten the screw to secure.

3. Apply glue to the back side of the inner hoop and finger-press the fabric in place to adhere it all around the circle.

4. Cut a 12" length of grosgrain ribbon from the 2½-yard length. Tie a bow and glue it to the upper edge of the hoop near the adjustment screw.

Assembling the Pocketed Board

1. Fold the pocket circle (without fleece) in half and press a crease line.

2. Unfold the circle and, following the manufacturer's instructions, fuse the interfacing to the wrong side of the circle, aligning it with the crease.

3. Refold the pocket and place the folded pocket over the fleece-backed circle's lower edge, matching the cut edges and noting any directional fabric patterning. Baste the layers together ¼" from the edge.

4. Based on what you plan to put into the pockets, mark pocket dividers accordingly from the lower circle edge to the upper pocket fold, keeping the lines perpendicular to the folded edge. Use chalk and a ruler to make sure your lines are straight.

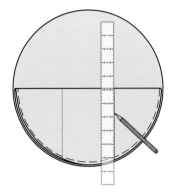

5. Beginning at the pocket lower edge, stitch along the marked divider lines; pivot and stitch one stitch parallel to the upper edge before stitching back down the length.

6. Follow steps 1–4 of "Assembling the Basic Board" on page 79 to complete.

Assembling the Ribboned Photo Board

1. Decide the arrangement of the crossed ribbons. Cut the lengths needed and pin them in place on the fleece-backed circle. Baste the ribbon ends ¼" from the circle edges.

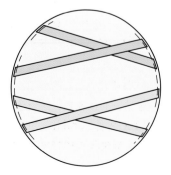

2. Follow steps 1–4 of "Assembling the Basic Board" on page 79 to complete.

3. Sew a button to each of the ribbon intersections through all layers; sew another one along the ribbon length.

Assembling the Chalkboard

1. Apply glue to the front surface of the inner hoop. Press the foam-board circle in place on top of the hoop and allow to dry.

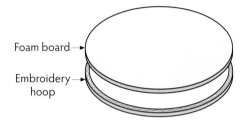

Foam board →

Embroidery → hoop

2. Apply glue to the outer edges of the inner hoop. Cover the foam board with the chalkboard-fabric circle. Apply glue to the inner edges of the outer hoop and place over the inner hoop. Tighten the hoop screw.

3. Trim the chalkboard fabric close to the hoop underside.

4. Thread 18" of ribbon through the chalk-holder clip and knot. Tie the opposite end to the embroidery-hoop adjuster.

5. Using 12" of ribbon, make a bow and glue to the upper hoop edge near the adjustment screw.

6. Before writing on the board, "season" it by rubbing chalk all over the surface and then wiping it off. Repeat. Use a damp cloth or an eraser to clean the board between uses.

Finishing

Use pins, clips, or clamps as desired to hold things in place on the boards.

coupon keeper

*K*eep your coupons in an organized fashion and have them ready to go when you are—no bulky binder needed! The keeper attaches to the handle of your shopping cart for an easy, hands-free shopping experience. Extra pockets provide room for your phone, pen, calculator, wallet, and more.

Designed and made by Heather Valentine.
Fabric from Hello Sunshine Cottons by Riley Blake Designs.
Finished size: 8" x 5½" x 2" excluding strap

Materials

Yardage is based on 42"-wide fabric unless otherwise noted. Fat quarters measure 18" x 21". Fat eighths measure 9" x 21".

⅜ yard of turquoise print for linings, strap, side pocket, and key loop
1 fat quarter of floral for outer bag (body, side panels, flap)
1 fat eighth of diagonal stripe for front pocket and side-pocket lining
1 yard of 22"-wide fusible fleece
Freezer paper or cardstock
Thin ponytail holder for button loop
1 button, ⅝" to ¾" diameter

Cutting

From the floral, cut:*
1 rectangle, 8¾" x 12¾" (bag body)
2 rectangles, 2¾" x 5¾" (side panels)
1 rectangle, 8½" x 9" (flap)

From the turquoise print, cut:*
1 rectangle, 8½" x 9" (flap)
1 piece, 4¾" x 23½" (strap)
1 rectangle, 1¾" x 3" (key loop)
1 rectangle, 2¾" x 3¾" (side pocket)
1 rectangle, 5⅜" x 7¾" (front pocket)
1 rectangle, 10¾" x 14¼" (lining)

From the diagonal stripe, cut:
1 rectangle, 2¾" x 4⅞" (side pocket)
1 rectangle, 4¼" x 7¾" (front pocket)

From the fusible fleece, cut:*
1 rectangle, 8½" x 9" (flap)
1 rectangle, 8¾" x 12¾" (body)
1 piece, 1¾" x 23½" (strap)
2 rectangles, 2¾" x 5¾" (side panel)

**Plan your cutting in advance and cut the largest pieces first.*

Preparing the Bag Sections

Use a ⅜" seam allowance throughout the construction of the coupon keeper unless instructed otherwise.

1. Make a template from freezer paper or cardstock using the flap-corner trimming pattern on page 85. Use it to round two corners of each floral, turquoise, and fusible-fleece 8½" x 9" piece.

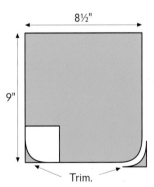

2. Iron the corresponding piece of fusible fleece to the wrong side of the floral flap, the floral 8¾" x 12¾" rectangle for the body, and the two floral 2¾" x 5¾" rectangles for the sides.

Adding Pockets

1. To make the front pocket, place the striped 4¼" x 7¾" rectangle and the turquoise print 5⅜" x 7¾" rectangle right sides together, aligning

them along one 7¾" edge. Stitch along the top edge and press the seam allowances toward the turquoise lining. Topstitch along the edge of the lining, next to the seam just sewn.

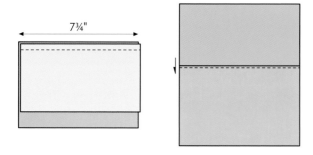

2. With right sides together, fold the pocket piece from step 1 so that the 7¾" edges align and press. Starting at the top edge, stitch along one side; turn at the corner and stitch for about 2". Repeat on the opposite side. Clip the corners; turn right side out and press.

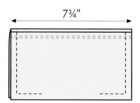

3. Position the pocket 1" below the 8¾" edge of the bag body and center it. Stitch along the sides and bottom. For extra stability, Heather likes to stitch a small triangle at each top corner.

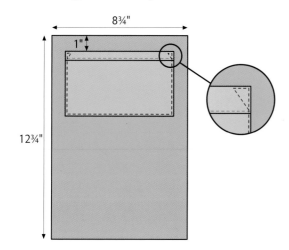

4. To make the side pocket, place the striped 2¾" x 4⅞" rectangle and the turquoise 2¾" x 3¾" rectangle right sides together, aligning them along one 2¾" edge. Stitch along the top edge and press the seam allowances toward the striped lining. Topstitch along the edge of the lining.

5. With right sides together, fold the pocket piece from step 4 so that the 3¾" edges align and press. Starting at the top edge, stitch down the side using a ¼" seam allowance. Repeat on the opposite side. The bottom edges will remain open.

6. To create the loop for keys, fold the turquoise 1¾" x 3" piece in half and press. Fold the raw edges in to the center crease, refold along the center crease, and press again. Add two rows of straight stitching, approximately ¼" apart.

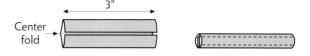

7. Pin the side pocket to one floral 2⅜" x 5¾" side panel. Pin the loop to the other side panel. Baste in place and remove the pins.

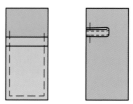

Assembling the Bag

1. Place the side panel with the pocket right sides together with the left side of the floral bag rectangle as shown. Pin the raw edges together and stitch along one side. When you're ⅜" from the corner, stop with the needle in the down position and pivot. Continue stitching across the bottom and pivot at the next corner; then stitch to the top. Repeat on the other side using the side panel with the loop. The loop should be on the right side of the bag and the side pocket should be on the left. Clip the seam allowance at the corners, being careful not to cut into the stitching.

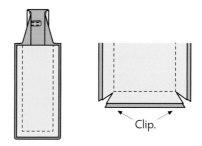

Clip.

2. Fold the ponytail holder in half; center and baste it in place along the bottom edge of the floral flap. Layer the flap lining and front right sides together. Stitch all around, leaving a 2½" opening along the straight short edge. Clip the corners, curves, and excess ponytail holder. Turn right side out and press. Topstitch ¼" from the edges all around.

3. Pin the flap to the back side of the bag, 1½" below the top edge. Stitch along the edge, and then again ¼" away. Backstitch at the beginning and end for reinforcement.

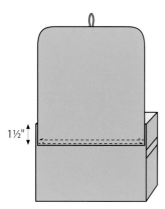

Adding the Strap

1. To create the strap, fuse the 1¾"-wide strip of fusible fleece to the center of the turquoise print 4¾" x 23½" strip. Fold and press one side of the strap fabric toward the center; fold and press a ¼" seam allowance on the opposite side; fold and press the fabric toward the center. Stitch along the center twice, spacing the rows of stitching ¼" apart.

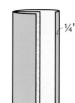
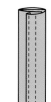

2. Position the strap 1½" below the top edge of the side panel and center it. Stitch in place ¼" from the edge. Fold the strap up and stitch again two times, ¼" apart. Repeat for the other end of the strap on the opposite side of the bag.

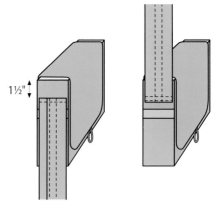

Finishing the Bag

1. Fold the turquoise 10¾" x 14¼" lining piece in half, right sides together, as shown. Straight stitch along one side of the lining. On the opposite side, stitch from the top edge to 1½" down. Repeat from the bottom up. Press and make a hard crease along the bottom edge.

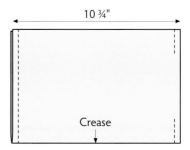

2. To create square corners in the lining, fold the side seam to align with the bottom crease. Draw a line 1" from the point and perpendicular to the side seam. Stitch on the line. Stitch again for reinforcement. Repeat on the other side. Press.

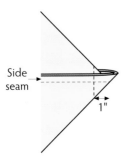

Side seam

1"

3. Insert the bag into the lining with right sides together. Tuck the strap and flap inside the lining, below the top of the bag and away from where you'll stitch. Stitch all around the top edge.

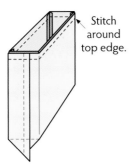

Stitch around top edge.

4. Turn the bag right side out through the opening in the lining. This will be a tight fit, so take your time and start by pulling out the strap and flap. Once everything is turned, use a blunt tool, such as a crochet hook, to push the seam allowances out and smooth the edges of the bag. Press.

5. Stitch the opening in the lining closed by hand or machine.

6. Take the coupon keeper on your next shopping trip and secure it to the shopping-cart handle by turning the flap to the back and attaching the ponytail holder to the button from the back.

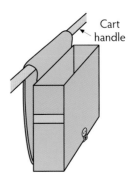

Cart handle

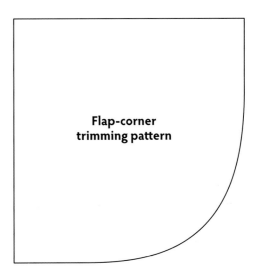

Flap-corner trimming pattern

coasters with curves

*D*o you want to add some fun and color to your home? Whip up these curvy coasters in an afternoon. Whether you use leftover strips from a favorite project or dig into a Jelly Roll, these coasters are a blast to make and are super absorbent because they're filled with cotton cording.

Designed and made by Jackie White.
Fabric from Flutter by Riley Blake Designs.
Finished size: 3¾" diameter

Materials for 4 Coasters

4 assorted print strips, 2½" x 42", for coasters
2 squares, 10" x 10", of coordinating print for backing
9 yards of cotton cording, ¼" diameter
2 yards of 1½"-wide red jumbo rickrack

Cutting

From *each* of the 4 strips, cut:
2 strips, 1¼" x 42" (8 total); cut each strip into
    4 strips, 1¼" x 10½"

From the cording, cut:
4 pieces, 80" long

From the rickrack, cut:
4 pieces, 18" long

Assembling the Coasters

1. Select eight 1¼" x 10½" strips and sew them right sides together along the 1¼" ends to make an 80½"-long strip. Make four.

2. Tack an 80" length of cording in place at the end of one of the fabric strips, centering it along the end. Place the cord in the middle of the strip and fold the fabric in half, wrong sides together. Sew along the raw edges with a ¼" seam allowance, encasing the cord in the middle. Use a zipper foot if you have one for your machine. You can stitch by hand as well. Make four.

3. Starting at one end, begin rolling the fabric-covered cording tightly into a circle. With needle and thread, tack by hand just below the stitched line. Continue until the strip is completely rolled and tack the end under the bottom. You may find it helpful to place it right side down on a flat surface as you coil and stitch with the wrong side up. Make four.

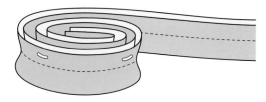

4. Place a coiled circle on the wrong side of one 10" square of fabric and trace around the outside of the circle. Repeat for each of the circles.

5. Place a second 10" square right sides together with the marked square and stitch ⅛" inside each of the traced circles. Cut out along the line, and then make a slit in one side and turn right side out. Make four.

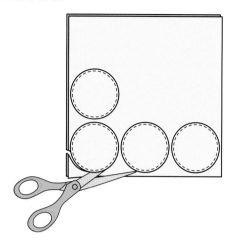

6. With the slit side of a circle facing up, pin one 18" length of rickrack along the edge of the circle with just ¼" of it catching the circle. Ease the rickrack so it lies flat as you go. Trim as needed and turn

the ends under. Stitch by hand or machine. Repeat for all four circles.

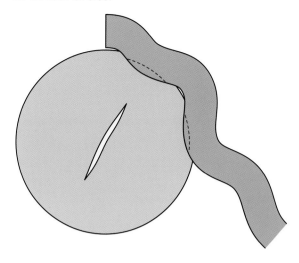

7. Place the coiled cording right side up on the slit side of the circle and hand stitch together. Repeat to make four coasters.

Tips and Ideas

- If the rickrack frays at the ends, dab on a bit of clear nail polish to stop the fraying.
- Make each coaster a different color so guests can tell them apart. You can use solids or prints.
- Instead of rickrack, use lace around the edge.

wine-glass charms and fridge magnets

*R*ickrack charms make it easy to serve your guests their beverages *without worrying about a mix-up. Make additional rickrack flowers without the loops and glue the colorful rosettes to magnets to dress up your message board or fridge. You can make them smaller or larger, whatever your preference. With just a bit of rickrack, you can stitch up a set in no time. The variety of colors is what makes these so much fun to make.*

Designed and made by Jackie White.
Finished size: 2" diameter

Materials for 4 Magnets or 4 Wine Charms

1¼ yards *each* of 4 colors of rickrack, ¾" wide, for flowers
5" x 5" square of coordinating fabric for flowers
5" x 5" square of cardboard for flowers
⅝ yard of narrow elastic cording for wine glass charms
1" x 6" piece of magnetic tape for fridge magnets
Hot-glue gun

Cutting

From the rickrack, cut:
8 pieces, 20" long (2 of each color)

From the 5" fabric square, cut:
4 circles, 2" diameter

From the cardboard, cut:
4 circles, 1" diameter

From the elastic, cut:
4 pieces, 5" long

Assembling the Flowers

1. Using one 20" piece each of two different colors of rickrack, align them so that the hill of one is on top of the valley of another. Place the pieces under your sewing machine and tack the ends together to hold them in place.

2. Twist the two pieces together over and under along their entire lengths. It will look like a rope when done. Machine stitch ⅛" from one long edge. Trim the ends even.

Spicy Sautéed Spinach

ACTIVE: 20 MINUTES; TOTAL: 20 MINUTES

6 SERVINGS For a little less heat, use fewer chiles or mustard seeds.

2 Tbsp. ghee (clarified butter) or
    vegetable oil
1 bunch scallions, coarsely chopped
2 dried chiles de árbol or ½ tsp.
    crushed red pepper flakes
2 garlic cloves, finely chopped
3 tsp. yellow mustard seeds
4 bunches flat-leaf spinach, stemmed,
    very coarsely chopped
    Kosher salt, freshly ground
    pepper

Heat ghee in a large skillet over medium-high heat. Add scallions, chiles, garlic, and mustard seeds. Cook, stirring often, until garlic begins to brown and mustard seeds pop, about 1 minute. Add spinach to skillet by the handful, allowing it to wilt between additions. Cook, tossing often, until spinach is tender, 5–6 minutes. Season with salt and pepper.

3. Fold one end of the rickrack over ¼" and use a hot-glue gun to add a dab of glue to hold. Begin rolling and adding little dabs of glue every ½" just above the stitching line.

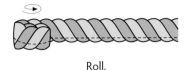

Roll.

4. When you reach the end, attach it to the bottom with glue. Repeat the steps to make four using different color combinations.

5. Sew a gathering stitch by hand ¼" in around the edge of one 2" fabric circle. Place a 1" cardboard circle on the wrong side of the fabric and gather the fabric around it. Tie a knot to secure.

Finishing for Fridge Magnets

1. Place the fabric-covered circle on the bottom of the rickrack flower with the gathered side next to the flower and glue in place with the hot-glue gun.

2. Cut a 1" circle from the magnetic strip and glue to the fabric-covered circle.

3. Starting from the outside edge, bend the rickrack back to open up the flower blossoms.

Finishing for Wine Charms

1. Bring the ends of the 5" length of elastic cording together and place them, centered, on the bottom of the rickrack flower. Glue in place with the hot-glue gun.

2. Place the fabric-covered circle on the bottom of the rickrack flower with the gathered side next to the flower and glue in place with the hot-glue gun.

3. Starting from the outside edge, bend the rickrack back to open up the flower blossoms.

Tips and Ideas

- Use a larger size of rickrack, such as 1" or 1½", to make a brooch or an embellishment for a bag.
- Use 30" lengths of rickrack to make your flowers bigger.
- Use ribbon elastic instead of elastic cording for the wine charms to give them a frilly look.

magnetic message board

A refrigerator can easily become cluttered with shopping lists, coupons, notes, and children's artwork. Save the most important items for this fabric-covered magnet board—ideal for organizing your kitchen.

Designed and made by Lindsay Conner.
Fabric is Ruby Star Sparkle by Melody Miller for Kokka.
Finished size: 16" x 20" outer frame; 12" x 16" opening

Materials

16" x 20" piece of fabric*
12" x 16" piece of galvanized sheet metal*
16" x 20" picture frame
Spray paint (optional)
Double-sided poster tape or spray adhesive (3M Super 77 Multipurpose Clear)
Duct tape
X-Acto knife or metal shears

For other sizes, add 4" to the length and width of the center of your frame. Sheet metal is available at hardware stores.

Preparing the Frame

Remove the backing board and glass from your frame. Spray paint the frame if desired, following the instructions on the can. Let dry completely.

Cutting the Sheet Metal

1. Mark the dimensions of the frame opening onto the galvanized sheet metal. You can use the glass as a pattern.

2. Score the marked lines 10 to 15 times with an X-Acto knife and snap off the excess. Or, cut the sheet metal with a pair of all-purpose shears, available at hardware stores.

3. Tape over the rough edges with duct tape.

Assembling the Board

1. Lay out the sheet metal in front of you. Center the fabric over one side of the sheet metal, with the right side facing up. Press the fabric smooth with an iron, folding the fabric around the edges of the metal to mark the edges. Turn the fabric and metal over and press each edge.

2. Remove the fabric and set it aside. Place double-sided tape around the perimeter of the sheet metal. Place several strips of tape vertically and horizontally through the center, making sure not to overlap or create any bubbles. Attach the fabric directly to the metal using the double-sided tape; or, you can use spray adhesive following the manufacturer's instructions.

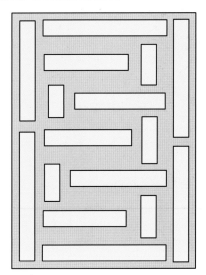

3. Wrap the excess fabric (2" on each side) around the back of the board like a present. Tape the fabric to the back of the metal with duct tape.

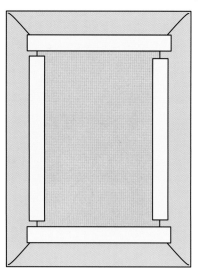

4. Place the fabric-covered metal in the frame and attach the backing board, or make one from heavy cardboard, and secure.

5. Hang the magnetic board on the wall and pair with strong magnets for an easy-to-use message station.

Finding a Frame

Look for interesting frames at estate sales, secondhand stores, and yard sales. Keep an eye out for ornate or oval frames for a striking look.

about the contributors

Natalie Barnes

Natalie is the owner of and designer for beyond the reef, a pattern-design company that she started in 1994 while drinking coffee on a lanai in Hanalei, Kauai. As a little girl, she learned to sew, knit, and crochet from her grandmother, and later began quilting with 99-cent Woolworth fabrics. After a successful career in the demanding commercial interior design field in Los Angeles, Natalie decided it was time to step out in faith, live her dream, and put her talents to work in another area. She has never looked back. Having always lived on the beach, her inspiration for color and design comes from the sea, the sky, and the land. These days, you'll also find her in the kitchen, making homemade dog biscuits for Buddy-dog! You can visit Natalie at www.beyondthereefpatterns.com.

Lindsay Conner

Lindsay is a writer, editor, and crafter who enjoys sewing original patterns for quilts, accessories, and home decor. She is the author of a quilting book, *Modern Bee: 13 Quilts to Make with Friends*. Her work has also been published in the *One-Yard Wonders* books, as well as *Stitch* and *Stitch Craft Create* magazines. Lindsay lives in Nashville, Tennessee, with her husband and quilt-loving cats, Murph and Chloe. You can follow her crafty ventures at LindsaySews.com and CraftBuds.com.

Melissa Corry

As a wife and a mother (she has five growing children), Melissa spends a large part of her day in the kitchen. Fortunately, it's one of her favorite places to be—after her sewing room, of course. She's thrilled to be part of this amazing book, which brings together two of her passions. To see more of Melissa's daily quilting and occasional cooking adventures, visit her blog: HappyQuiltingMelissa.blogspot.com.

Jenifer Dick

Jenifer began quilting in 1993 when, on a whim, she signed up for a beginning quiltmaking class. From that first stitch she was hooked. Since 2001, she's been speaking to guilds and teaching quiltmaking. She's authored four books on topics from traditional to modern quilts, and has been published in many other books and magazines. Jenifer lives in Harrisonville, Missouri, with her husband and three children. Follow her blog at 42quilts.com.

Amy Ellis

Amy was amazed to discover the great source of inspiration and abundance of knowledge that makes up the blogging world, and decided to become part of it. Via Amy's Creative Side, she shares current projects (including quilts, bags, and the occasional garment), product reviews, and little bits of her family life as a wife and mother. She hosts a biannual Bloggers' Quilt Festival, where there's no judging or required skill set for entry, so it's more like a big party online! Amy is the author of three books and this is her third time as a contributor. Visit her blog at AmysCreativeSide.com.

Linda Turner Griepentrog

Linda loves all thing fabric and fiber—just look in her sewing room and closets! Since graduating from Oregon State University, she's had a varied career in the sewing industry. As a designer, writer, and editor, she works with several companies in the sewing, crafting, and quilting communities. Linda is the author of five books and thousands of magazine articles. She loves to solve sewing challenges and believes that, given enough time and thought, she can construct anything! Linda, her husband (conveniently, a fabric-store manager), and three dogs live in Bend, Oregon.

Kim Niedzwiecki

Kim, also known as Go-Go Kim, lives in a home filled with sewing items everywhere; if you look closely under the fabric piles, you may even find a child or two! A mom of four and grandmother of two, she juggles her time between mom taxi and that next sewing project. Kim has created patterns and tutorials that you can find online at Pellon Projects (pellonprojects .com), Moda Bake Shop (modabakeshop.com), and her blog, My Go-Go Life (gogokim.blogspot.com). Kim dearly loves her blog since it has connected her to many other wonderful friends who love to sew.

Kari Ramsay

Quilt and pattern designer Kari of Fresh Cut Quilts has been pursuing art and design nearly all her life. As a child she loved to sit at her mother's side and watch her paint and sew. Kari soon began learning to paint from her mom, and then continued on to sewing lessons. Her passion for creative design has continued throughout her life. Fresh Cut Quilts began in 2007 with little more than a few designs and a big dream. She named her business Fresh Cut as a play on words based on her love of floral design, flowers, and her idea that quilts should be "fresh" and unique. Many of her designs are also inspired by her collection and love of vintage textiles. She lives in the shadow of the Rocky Mountains in Utah with her husband and children. You can find her patterns and fabrics online at FreshCutQuilts.com.

Missy Shepler

Missy is the coauthor of *The Complete Idiot's Guide to Sewing*. Whenever possible, Missy combines her day job as a designer, author, and illustrator with her love of stitching by creating projects, patterns, and illustrations for sewing and quilting clients and publications. See what she's currently stitching at MissyStitches.com.

Rebecca Silbaugh

With a lifelong passion for art and design, a career in graphic design seemed fitting, but that all changed after Rebecca helped out at her mother's quilt shop. The fabrics, the colors, the textures—they all won over her heart and inspired her to design quilts. Armed with a pencil and some graph paper, the ideas began to work themselves onto paper from her mind, which led to the opening of Ruby Blue Quilting Studio in the fall of 2009. Today, the company has evolved into a multifaceted creative outlet for Rebecca, including online tutorials, several patterns, and long-arm quilting services. Rebecca currently lives in Madison, Ohio, just minutes from Lake Erie, with her husband, Ben, and their two dogs, Duncan and Paco. Aside from quilting, you can also find Rebecca in her garden or traveling with her husband. Visit her at RubyBlueQuilts.blogspot.com.

Amy Struckmeyer

Amy lives just outside of Chicago with her husband and two strong-willed and creative children. Her love for textiles began early in her Waldorf School education with lessons in knitting, weaving, and sewing. An architect by profession, she now uses her design and drawing skills to create modern sewing projects and patterns, some of which have appeared in *Stitch* magazine. She recently fell in love with screen printing and wishes she had the space to properly print yards of fabric. One of these days, she just might sew her first quilt. Visit her at FormWorkDesign.blogspot.com.

Heather Valentine

Heather is the creative juice behind the Sewing Loft, a sewing community focused on inspiring you to reclaim your creativity, one stitch at a time. After earning a degree in fashion design and pattern making from New York's Fashion Institute of Technology, Heather took her talent to some of the top name brands in the apparel industry. In addition to designing patterns, she shares her creative process and sewing tips and tricks with the community on her blog: TheSewingLoft.com.

Jackie White

Jackie is a mother of two young boys and married to a wonderful man who has learned more about quilting than he ever imagined. Her passion is creating three-dimensional art quilts. Jackie has worked long and hard in this field, and is now branching out to teach workshops and give lectures and trunk shows on her techniques. Her work has been juried into shows across North America. She also writes for two publications, one being a humorous column on quilting. When she's not in her studio making three-dimensional art quilts, you can find her at her blog: Jabotquilt.blogspot.ca.